COUNTRY INNS
AND BACK ROADS
COOKBOOK

Recipes from inns featured in
Country Inns and Back Roads, North America

THE BERKSHIRE TRAVELLER PRESS
Stockbridge, Massachusetts

SELECTED BERKSHIRE TRAVELLER PRESS TITLES:

Country Inn Cookbook
Treasured Recipes of Country Inns
Apple Orchard Cookbook
Diners of the Northeast
Country Inns and Back Roads, North America
Country Inns and Back Roads, Britain and Ireland
Measured Drawings of Shaker Furniture
Practical Plans for Barns, Carriage Houses,
    Stables and Other Country Buildings

Cover Painting by Nancy Simpson
Designed and Illustrated by Janice Lindstrom

Library of Congress Catalog Card Number: 79-52080
ISBN 0-912-94456-0

Printed in Dalton, Massachusetts, U.S.A. by The Studley Press, Inc.

15 14 13 12 11 10 9 8 7 6 5 4 3 2 1

*To all those country-inn-goers
who ever wanted the recipe
for that special dish, but
were afraid to ask*

FOREWORD

This is the third book of recipes gathered from the country inns featured in my book, *Country Inns and Back Roads, North America.* It hardly seems possible that the first book, *Country Inn Cookbook,* was published in 1968; the second was entitled *Treasured Recipes of Country Inns,* and they are both still in print. The recipes in this entirely new book were chosen from several submitted by each inn, and the selection was made on the basis of the recipe's being representative of the individual inn, and also with an eye to developing a balanced cookbook.

There was a time when the traveler stopping at a country inn would find meals that reflected the produce and cookery of the region. For instance, in New England the fare would most likely include fish stews, clam chowders, boiled dinners, pot roasts, and Indian puddings; whereas a traveler in Virginia or South Carolina would dine on peanut soup, southern fried chicken, baked ham, black-eyed peas, and spoon bread. Today, it is quite a different story. In some country inns the visitor will find the cuisine to be decidedly French; in others there is a gourmet cook whose specialties may range from Oriental to Austrian dishes. There are still a few inns where the meals are representative of their locales. This cookbook offers a sampling from all varieties of country inn cookery.

We are indebted to Brenda Everett for a great deal of the preliminary work in setting up a standard form. Virginia Rowe performed further editing and coordination which involved being in touch, sometimes more than once, with various inns to make certain each recipe was precise and correct. Janice Lindstrom's illustrations and designs have enhanced many of our books, and we appreciate her fine contributions.

I hope that you'll enjoy these recipes and that you'll visit some of these inns.

Norman Simpson

A Short, Lively History of the American Country Inn

The American country inn, along with the church and the New England town meeting, ranks as one of the oldest continuing institutions in our country. Town records from the mid-17th century indicate that many communities were required by law to provide some type of accommodations and provender for travelers by whatever name they might be called—inn, ordinary, hostelry, or what-have-you.

The American Colonial inn was kept by an innkeeper and his family and was the center of village activity. Those early inns also temporarily served as churches, gaols, blockhouses, court-rooms, and hospitals. Their *alter egos* include lecture halls, theaters, mortuaries, bordellos, runaway slave stations, grist mills, ferry stops, mountain shelters, smugglers' hideaways, and political campaign headquarters.

Inns were established in villages in the 17th and 18th centuries when travel was by foot or horseback; however, many later inns had their beginnings as stagecoach and freight wagon stops. Inns were also built on the great toll roads like the "National Pike." During the developmental years of our country, innkeeping moved west along with the settlers, and the tradition of finding refuge and food in ranches and cabins on the prairies and in the mountains later turned many a farm and ranch into an inn.

Although its real development was to come many years later, the precedent for the American resort was established in Colonial days when a royal governor grew weary of the heat and humidity in Boston, and began a summer colony high in the New Hampshire mountains. The American resort-inn was born. As early as Washington's youth some people started to follow the European custom of journeying to the numerous mineral springs.

In the early part of the 19th century, railroads replaced the stagecoach, and the American inn at stagestops began to disappear. As the century moved forward, small towns grew up along the railroads and travelers stayed at what became known as commercial hotels. By the last quarter of the century the railroads encouraged the vacation concept. Riding the "steam cars" on twin tracks that were frequently engineering marvels, families from the city would travel to the mountains, seashore, and mineral springs resorts to spend many weeks during the summer. Tremendous hotels requiring large staffs were built and for 75 years these were a significant part of the American vacation scene. These in turn were augmented by local farms in the vicinity who took in boarders.

In the early 1920s the railroads were displaced by the automobile, which made Americans more mobile and gradually changed vacation and holiday styles from summer-long stays to a few days or a weekend. One by one the large resort hotels disappeared, although the smaller, summer boarding houses and farms adapted themselves more readily to the shorter stays. In the 1950s these would emerge in importance, particularly with the development of the ski vacation.

The automobile awakened an insatiable desire to travel in Americans. All over the country, the signs "Guests" and "Tourist Home" could be seen in the windows of private homes. The American version of European "bed and breakfast" was keeping the spirit of personal innkeeping alive. It became quite a popular pastime for families to load up the car and see where the road would take them. Travel was fun and although at first the tires were rim changers, repair shops infrequent, and the road often muddy, the great American love affair with the automobile was well under way.

Salesmen and business people, who had previously made great use of the railroads, now bought a Ford or a Dodge and started making business trips by automobile. Now a new accommodation concept developed—the motel, or motor hotel. The railroad, like the stagecoach, began to disappear, and with it the small commercial hotel.

The new travel fad, the motel, displaced the tourist home and the chain motel came into being wherein prefabricated buildings could be erected in a relatively short time and the mass-produced accommodations had many advantages: quick reservation systems, readily accessible rooms, telephones and TV, a casual informality in dress, and a certain standardization of design and decoration. The European visitor to America could travel all over the country, stay in motels, but perhaps wonder in the morning whether he were in Wichita or Chattanooga.

Meanwhile, the American country inns that had survived 150 years of changing travel styles, now almost faded from sight. True, here and there, there were some inns located on main highways that made adjustments and added a few features that might make them competitive with nearby motels. They even constructed motel units as a concession to the motoring-conscious public. However, most of them had been converted to other uses or torn down to make way for gasoline stations, supermarkets, or even motels. In the 1950s there was a mere handful of country inns in existence.

Looking back, I believe it was about the middle of the 1960s when the renaissance of the American country inn began. A small but growing segment of the American traveling and vacationing public began searching for an alternative to the efficient but impersonal style of motel traveling. They began to "discover" the antithesis of the large motel—the country inn, where personalized innkeeping, individually furnished rooms, home-cooked food, quiet countryside surroundings, and an atmosphere that included living rooms and parlors with book-shelves and fireplaces, encouraged conversation with new friends. These inns were not found on the interstates, but on the meandering lesser roads. In many respects the country inn became a tangible symbol of the American search for some of the desirable virtues of the past.

It was a slow process at first, but many wonderful things began to happen. For example, some of the inns of the 18th and 19th centuries that had been converted to other uses came back into their own. False ceilings were ripped away revealing beautiful, heavy beams. Walls were removed to disclose hand-some fireplaces. Layers of wallpaper were carefully peeled away to reveal beautiful 18th-century stenciling. Many buildings were saved from being torn down literally in the knick of time. Furthermore, as country inns grew in popularity we were all amazed at how well they adapted to their original use!

Perhaps best of all, many American communities without village inns or small hotels since the late Victorian days, now found new vigor and pride in their own restored inns.

In the 1960s and '70s a new genre of innkeepers came into being. These were men and women who had been successful in other occupations and were attracted to the idea of moving to the country with their families in order to find a new way of life. Usually they had been guests in several country inns and found that the idea of owning one was something that appealed to their sense of adventure. They are dedicated, intelligent, eager to learn, adaptable, friendly, and most of all, they really like people. Many participate in active outdoor sports like tennis and skiing. They enjoy the idea of operating an inn as they would their own home, and many have furnished their inns with their own personal antiques. Some have had practical experience in the hospitality field and a few have even attended hotel schools. On the other hand, many began as enthusiastic amateurs.

They all agree that they have not found it a bed of roses. Innkeeping is a very hard master. Long hours, economic conditions, the weather, the energy crisis, and government regulations all contribute to make the going very rough at times.

True American innkeeping (which flickered, but was never really extinguished) now burns brighter than ever. I have discovered inns in villages where the great attraction is beautiful homes and gardens, tree-lined streets, antique shops, and museums. Still other inns have evolved as a result of being located in the mountains or next to the seashore. In many cases the country boarding house became an inn. Many inns have grown up near centers of active sports such as tennis, golf, horseback riding, and skiing. Several inns include many different combinations, as Americans prove how varied and subtle are their recreational tastes and preferences.

CONTENTS

SALADS

FISH AND SHELLFISH

FISH AND SHELLFISH (Cont'd.)

POULTRY AND GAME

MEATS

MEATS (Cont'd.)

BRUNCH AND LUNCHEON DISHES (Cont'd.)

BREADS

CAKES

CAKES (Cont'd.)

PUDDINGS

PIES

PIES (Cont'd.)

DESSERTS AND SAUCES

CONDIMENTS AND JAMS

APPETIZERS

ALGONQUIN HOTEL

THE REDCOAT'S RETURN·

CHESTER INN

WALNUT MUSHROOMS STUFFED WITH OX TONGUE IN SOUR SAUCE

ALGONQUIN HOTEL, New York, New York

For the warmth and personal hospitality of a country inn in the middle of New York City, go to the Algonquin. This small hotel is the favorite of all kinds of interesting people who have a variety of reasons for loving it, not the least of which is the food.

60 medium-sized mushrooms (about 1 1/2 lbs.)
salt
lemon juice
6 oz. cream cheese, softened
2/3 pt. sour cream
1/2 cup Dijon-type mustard
1 4 to 6-lb. cooked ox tongue, finely chopped
60 shelled walnut halves

Preheat the oven to 350°. Remove stems and clean mushrooms. Place mushroom caps in a large shallow ovenproof dish; sprinkle with salt and lemon juice. Bake 10 to 15 minutes. Chill.

Combine cream cheese, sour cream and mustard into a smooth sauce. Gently mix the chopped ox tongue with the sour cream and spoon the mixture into the chilled, blanched mushroom caps. Top each stuffed mushroom with a walnut half. Serve on a platter centered with a small bowl of salted walnuts. Yield: 60 stuffed mushrooms.

HAM AND CHEESE BEIGNETS

THE REDCOAT'S RETURN, Tannersville, New York

The innkeepers of this Catskill Mountain hideaway a few miles from Tannersville, Tom and Peggy Wright, fled Manhattan's canyons of steel in 1972. Tom, who is the chef, is a Londoner who formerly cooked on some of the great transAtlantic liners. As he says, "Today, England is ten minutes from Tannersville."

1/2 cup butter
1 cup water
1/2 tsp. salt
1 3/4 cups flour
6 eggs
1 cup finely diced Swiss cheese
1 cup finely diced ham
oil for deep frying
parsley sprigs for garnish

In a 3-quart saucepan melt the butter and add the water and salt. When the mixture boils add the flour and stir it quickly with a wooden spoon until the batter leaves the sides of the pan. Remove from the heat and add the eggs one at a time, beating well after each addition. Mix in the diced cheese and ham.

Heat oil for deep frying until it reaches 375° on a deep frying thermometer. Drop Beignet batter by the teaspoonful into the hot oil, frying a few at a time. Remove the Beignets to a heated platter as they become golden brown. Serve on a heated dish with a paper doily; garnish with parsley sprigs. Serves 6.

LOVETT'S BY LAFAYETTE BROOK

PUMP HOUSE

HOMESTEAD INN

SALMON MOUSSE

LOVETT'S BY LAFAYETTE BROOK, Franconia, New Hampshire

A fine example of an early American farmhouse, this sophisticated country inn offers its guests gourmet meals and excellent service in the midst of the White Mountains resort area. Here's one of the super dishes Charlie Lovett has cooked up in his dandy kitchen.

2 cups flaked, poached
  fresh salmon
1 tbsp. butter
1 tbsp. flour
1/2 cup milk
1/2 tbsp. dry mustard
salt
pinch cayenne pepper
1 package unflavored
  gelatin
3 tbsp. white wine or water
1 cup heavy cream,
  whipped and lightly
  salted
lettuce for garnish
mayonnaise
fresh lemon juice
chopped fresh dill

Force the flaked salmon through a sieve or purée in a food processor. Transfer to a large mixing bowl. In a small saucepan, prepare a white sauce: Melt the butter and whisk in the flour. Continue to cook, whisking constantly, until mixture begins to bubble. Meanwhile, in a separate saucepan, heat the milk. When flour paste begins to bubble, stir in the hot milk and continue to cook, stirring, until sauce thickens. Bring to a boil, lower heat and cook 2 to 3 minutes longer. Cool. Season the white sauce with mustard, salt to taste and cayenne pepper. Soften gelatin in the wine and dissolve over hot water. Mix the white sauce with the salmon and add dissolved gelatin. Combine thoroughly and chill. When the mixture begins to set, fold in the whipped cream. Transfer to 12 individual molds or a 2-quart ring mold and chill. Combine mayonnaise with lemon juice and chopped dill. Serve on lettuce and garnish with dilled mayonnaise. Yield: 12 appetizers or 6 main courses.

SEVICHE OF SCALLOPS

PUMP HOUSE, Canadensis, Pennsylvania

This is a sophisticated inn with an ambience and cuisine that have received accolades from many well-known publications, including Gourmet magazine and the New York Times. Chef Mark Kaplan wishes you "Bon appetit" with his following recipe.

3 cups small bay scallops
1 medium-sized red
  onion, thinly sliced
1 large red pepper, seeded
  and cut into thin strips
1 large green pepper,
  seeded and cut into thin
  strips
juice of 3 oranges
juice of 2 lemons
juice of 2 limes
salt to taste
cayenne pepper to taste
3 shallots, peeled and
  diced

In a glass bowl, combine all ingredients and cover. Refrigerate at least 24 hours before serving. The Seviche should be spicy and only the freshest of scallops should be used in its preparation. Serve in champagne glasses, scallop shells, or avocado halves, and garnish with slices of the same fruits used in marinade. Serves 6.

CLAMS DES GOURMETS

HOMESTEAD INN, Greenwich, Connecticut
Haute cuisine *is the rule rather than the exception at this chic country inn located just a few miles north of New York City on the Connecticut coast. Each of the thirteen guest rooms is splendidly furnished with many antiques. This recipe is for one of Chef Jacques Theibeult's more popular dishes.*

6 large clams
18 tsp. Duxelles (below)
1/2 cup Herb Butter
** (below)**

Prepare Duxelles and Herb Butter. Preheat oven to 350°. Open clams, place about 3 teaspoons Duxelles on each clam and top with Herb Butter. Bake 5 to 8 minutes. Yield: 6 stuffed clams.

DUXELLES:

1 lb. mushrooms
3 tbsp. butter

In a food processor or by hand, chop mushrooms as finely as possible. In a medium-sized skillet, melt butter and cook mushrooms over low heat until they are reduced to a paste.

HERB BUTTER:

1/4 lb. butter, softened
3 cloves garlic, finely
** chopped**
2 shallots, finely chopped
1/4 cup finely chopped
** parsley**
salt
freshly ground black
** pepper**

In a mixing bowl, combine softened butter, garlic, shallots, and parsley. Mix thoroughly and season to taste with salt and pepper.

HOT ARTICHOKE HORS D'OEUVRES WITH PITA BREAD

GOOSE COVE LODGE, Deer Isle, Maine
Goose Cove Lodge has 2500 feet on Goose Cove. All of the sleeping accommodations, located in attractive, rustic cabins, have their own sun decks, living rooms with fireplaces, and gorgeous sea views. Such an atmosphere naturally creates voracious appetites and here's a sample from Elli Pavloff's kitchen.

1 can artichoke hearts,
** drained**
1/2 cup mayonnaise
1/2 cup Parmesan cheese
Worcestershire sauce, to
** taste**
pinch coarse pepper
pita bread, toasted (below)

Preheat oven to 400°. In a food processor with a steel blade, place all ingredients, except the bread, and blend just a few seconds until artichokes are coarsely chopped. Put in small casserole and heat in oven until bubbling and slightly golden brown on top. Meanwhile, prepare pita bread. This spread can be used with crackers, also. Yield: 2 1/2 cups.

PITA BREAD:

1 clove garlic, crushed
1/2 cup butter, softened
1 pita bread
1/2 tsp. ground oregano
1/4 cup Parmesan cheese

In a small bowl, thoroughly mix garlic and butter. Cut open the pita bread and spread garlic butter on each half. Sprinkle with oregano and Parmesan cheese. With kitchen scissors, cut each half into 8 pie-shaped wedges. Place on cookie sheet and toast in hot oven until golden brown. Yield: 16 wedges of pita toast.

CRAB IMPERIAL

THE SEA HUT, Palmetto, Florida
Longtime devotees of the Red Inn in Provincetown, Cape Cod, will be delighted to know that the Barker family has now opened this unusual restaurant on the shores of Pelican Point in Palmetto. Besides an extensive menu of seafood offerings, they also have such main dishes as chicken Baltimore and frogs' legs.

12 oz. lump meat of the
  blue crab (or substitute
  lobster or king
  crabmeat)
1/2 cup Imperial Sauce
  (below)

Preheat oven to 450°. Remove any bone or tissue in blue crabmeat. In a medium-sized bowl combine crabmeat and sauce; divide evenly in four 4- or 5-ounce ramekins. Bake 8 to 10 minutes or until light brown and bubbly.

IMPERIAL SAUCE:

1 tbsp. butter
1 tbsp. flour
3/4 cup milk
2 cup mayonnaise
1 tbsp. Worcestershire
1/4 tsp. salt
1/4 tsp. Tabasco
1 egg, beaten

In a 2-quart saucepan, over medium heat, melt butter; slowly stir in flour and whisk about 5 minutes. Gradually add milk and cook just until thick. Cool completely. Then add mayonnaise, Worcestershire, salt, and Tabasco, combining thoroughly. Fold in beaten egg. This sauce may be stored in a tightly-covered container in the refrigerator up to three weeks. Yield: 3 cups.

ESCARGOTS MAISON

CHESTER INN, Chester, Vermont
Rocking on the front porch is one of the favorite pastimes in this central Vermont inn. It comes as a surprise to many a first-time guest that the menu features many sophisticated French dishes, including this tempting appetizer.

MARINADE:

1 8-oz. can of snails
1 bay leaf
4 cloves garlic
4 shallots
1/4 tbsp. dried chervil
1/4 tbsp. basil
1 medium onion,
  quartered
2 tbsp. olive oil
1/2 cup white wine
Rind of 1 orange

Combine liquid from can of snails with all ingredients in medium-sized saucepan, bring to a boil and pour over the snails. The marinade should just cover the snails. Refrigerate the snails in the marinade for 24 hours.

GARLIC BUTTER:

1 lb. butter, softened
1/4 cup parsley
2 cups chopped cooked
  spinach
4 shallots, finely chopped
4 cloves garlic, crushed

Combine all ingredients in medium-sized mixing bowl.

Remove snails from marinade.

Place snails in shells and fill any empty place in shell with garlic butter to cover. Heat under broiler in ovenproof serving dish for 4 minutes or until sizzling. Yield: 6 appetizer servings.

DUCK LIVER PASTE

SCHUMACHER'S NEW PRAGUE INN, New Prague, Minnesota
Nancy and John Schumacher are representative of a dedicated genre of new younger innkeepers who gain great satisfaction and personal fulfillment in running a country inn. This one resembles inns and hotels I have visited in Bavaria and Austria. The menu has a startling total of 55 main dishes available, and this is one of the great favorites.

2 pts. duck livers
1 pt. water
1 large onion, chopped
1 bay leaf
1 cup (8 oz.) cream cheese,
  softened
1/2 cup mayonnaise
salt
freshly ground black
  pepper

Wash livers and place in a medium-sized saucepan with water, onion, and bay leaf. Simmer 45 minutes to 1 hour. Drain and discard bay leaf. In a blender or food processor, grind the liver and onion mixture to a smooth paste. Add cream cheese and mayonnaise and combine thoroughly. Season to taste with salt and pepper. Chill. Yield: 3 cups duck liver paste.

SOUPS

ASTICOU INN

BRAMBLE INN

CHESHIRE INN

TURTLE SOUP

ASTICOU INN, Northeast Harbor, Maine

In the late 1920s and early '30s the American novelist Willa Cather enjoyed a magnificent view of Northeast Harbor from the spacious deck of this gracious inn, which is only open during the summer months. It is located most conveniently for an extended Mount Desert holiday. Many's the compliment Chef Allen Weigman has received for this soup.

4 stalks celery, finely
  chopped
2 large onions, finely
  chopped
2 lbs. frozen turtle meat
1 1/4 cup vegetable oil
2 qts. water
2 oz. essence of beef
1 4-oz. can tomatoes,
  crushed
1 bunch parsley, finely
  chopped
1 cup flour
juice of 3 lemons
1/3 cup dry sherry
salt
freshly ground black
  pepper
Worcestershire sauce
thin lemon slices
sieved hard-cooked egg
  for garnish

Partially defrost and cube turtle meat. In a heavy stockpot sauté celery, onion, and turtle meat in 1/4 cup of the vegetable oil until turtle meat is tender. Add water and essence of beef. Bring to a full boil. Add crushed tomatoes and chopped parsley. In another pot or skillet combine the flour and remaining cup of oil and stir with a whisk to make a smooth roux. Add the roux to the soup and heat through. Add lemon juice and sherry and season to taste with salt, pepper and Worcestershire. Serve the soup garnished with lemon slices and sieved egg. Serves 8.

COLD SUMMER SQUASH SOUP

BRAMBLE INN, Brewster, Massachusetts

Karen Etsell and Elaine Brenman have fashioned not only a tiny inn, but also an exciting art gallery in this quiet town on the north shore of Cape Cod. It's a refreshing experience, and this soup is typical of the tasty meals.

2 tbsp. butter
8 green onions, chopped
6 summer squash,
  chopped
3 cups chicken stock
pinch freshly grated
  nutmeg
salt
freshly ground black
  pepper
2 cups light cream
chopped fresh parsley for
  garnish

In a 3-quart saucepan, melt butter and sauté the scallions until they are golden. Add squash and stock and cook 15 minutes or until squash is tender. Transfer to a blender and purée. Add nutmeg, salt, and pepper to taste and light cream. Chill. Serve cold garnished with chopped fresh parsley. Serves 8.

BURGERSHIRE SOUP

CHESHIRE INN, St. Louis, Missouri
Here's a touch of Merry Olde England right on the outskirts of St. Louis. This hearty soup, served everyday at the inn, would be as appropriate in London as it is here where there are two red British double-decker buses parked at the entrance.

1 tbsp. vegetable oil
3/4 lb. lean ground beef
1 1/4 cups boiling beef
   stock
1 cup chopped onion
1/2 cup diced carrots
1/2 cup diced celery
1/2 cup canned tomatoes,
   crushed
1 tsp. salt
1/2 tsp. sugar
1/4 tsp. freshly ground
   black pepper
1 tbsp. flour
2 1/2 tbsp. cooked pearl •
   barley
3/4 tsp. Kitchen Bouquet

In a heavy 3-quart stock pot heat the vegetable oil and lightly brown the ground beef. Do not overcook or crumble the beef. Pour in the hot stock. Add the vegetables and seasonings. Cover and simmer until vegetables are barely tender. Skim the fat from the soup and reserve. In a skillet combine the reserved fat and the flour and brown the mixture, stirring constantly. Add one cup of stock to the flour mixture in the skillet and cook, stirring constantly, until clear. Return the contents of the skillet to the stock pot. Add cooked barley and Kitchen Bouquet, heat, and taste for correct seasoning. Serves 6.

CREAM OF CHICKEN CUCUMBER ONION SOUP

THE COUNTRY INN, Berkeley Springs, West Virginia
Even though it's in the middle of the town, a small brook must be crossed to reach the front door of this southern colonial mansion, with its red brick exterior and white two-story-high pillars. Guests come from miles away to sample this unusual Sunday specialty.

2 cucumbers, peeled,
   diced
2 small onions, peeled,
   diced
1/2 cup butter
2 cups water
2 10-oz. cans cream of
   chicken soup
2 cups milk
1 tsp. curry powder
salt
white pepper

In a heavy 3 to 4-quart saucepan, cook cucumbers, onions, and butter in water until soft. Add soup, milk, curry powder, and salt and white pepper to taste. Heat to a strong simmer, stirring frequently. Serves 8.

THE COUNTRY INN

BLACK POINT INN

GRANDVIEW FARM

SPALDING INN CLUB

MARYLAND INN

CLAREMONT HOTEL

ICED LEMON SOUP

SPALDING INN CLUB, Whitefield, New Hampshire

One of the last great New Hampshire White Mountain inns, this elegant resort-inn is a center for lawn bowling in New England. This soup would be a wonderful way to start a dinner party on a warm summer night.

5 cups chicken stock
grated rind of 4 lemons,
 plus juice of 4 lemons
2 tbsp. butter
2 tbsp. flour
1/2 cup sugar
4 tbsp. lemon extract
1 pt. heavy cream

In a large saucepan, bring chicken stock to a boil; add half the lemon rind and the lemon juice and boil 5 minutes longer. Meanwhile, in a small saucepan, in a small amount of water, boil the remaining rind until soft, strain and reserve the rind. When the chicken stock has boiled 5 minutes, strain it, discarding the rind. In another large saucepan, melt the butter, then whisk in the flour and cook 2 to 3 minutes, whisking constantly. Pour in the hot chicken stock and, stirring, add sugar and lemon extract. Continue to cook 5 to 8 minutes until sugar is dissolved. Chill. Add heavy cream and strain the soup through cheese-cloth or a very fine strainer. Serve in chilled bowls garnished with the reserved rind, powdered sugar, or sour cream. Serves 6.

CRAB BISQUE

MARYLAND INN, Annapolis, Maryland

Dating back to well before the American Revolution this ancient hostelry, in one of the country's most picturesque seaport towns, can boast of playing host to many of the important figures in American history. Today it is well-known for its highly imaginative menu which includes many dishes whose origins are in the nearby Chesapeake Bay waters.

1 qt. milk
2 tbsp. butter
1 tbsp. chicken base
2 tbsp. cornstarch
2 tbsp. half-&-half
1/4 tsp. pepper
1/2 tsp. celery salt
1/4 tsp. mustard
1/2 tsp. Old Boy seasoning
1/3 cup crabmeat
1/4 cup sherry

In a large saucepan, bring to a boil milk, butter, and chicken base. In a small bowl, combine the cornstarch and half-&-half, mixing until smooth, and add to the boiling milk, stirring constantly. Add seasonings and continue cooking for 10 minutes, stirring occasionally. Just before serving, add crabmeat and the sherry. Serves 6.

MAINE SHRIMP STEW

CLAREMONT HOTEL, Southwest Harbor, Maine
The oldest continuously operating hotel on Mount Desert Island, the Claremont was built in 1884 and many succeeding generations of the same families have been coming back ever since. Although we have this recipe in Soups, in Maine a shellfish stew is considered a main dish.

4 tbsp. butter
2 cups small shrimp
6 cups milk
salt
freshly ground black
  pepper

Peel and steam shrimp. In a heavy 3-quart stock pot, melt butter, then sauté shrimp 5 minutes over medium heat. Add milk and heat the stew, but do not boil. Season to taste with salt and pepper. Serves 6.

YELLOW SPLIT PEA SOUP

INN AT HUNTINGTON, Huntington, Massachusetts
Murray Schuman is an academic chef, an artist who is equally at home in his own spotless kitchen and in the classroom. He and his wife Barbara, along with their two junior innkeepers, Hans and Aaron, are holding forth at this delightful restaurant located in the hill country of western Massachusetts.

1 lb. yellow split peas
2 qts. chicken stock or
  water
butter
1 large onion, diced
1 large carrot, diced
1 large stalk celery, diced
4 oz. smoked sausage
  (kielbasa), ham, or
    knockwurst, diced
salt
freshly ground black
  pepper
pinch ground summer
  savory

Pour small quantities of dried peas onto a white plate and sort to make sure no pebbles are included with the peas. When all the peas have been sorted, rinse them under cold water. In a 3- to 4-quart pot, bring stock or water to a boil. Add peas. Reduce heat and simmer 1 1/2 to 2 hours. In a lidded skillet melt enough butter to coat bottom of the pan, add the diced vegetables, cover and cook over moderate heat until barely tender, 3 to 5 minutes. When the peas are tender, add the cooked diced vegetables and sausage and continue to cook 15 minutes stirring frequently. Season to taste with salt and pepper (adding more water or stock if soup is too thick; cook longer and stir vigorously if too thin). Add summer savory with discretion; must not be dominant flavor. Serves 10.

BROCCOLI BLUE SOUP

GRANDVIEW FARM, Huntsville, Ontario, Canada
Diners at this Ontario resort inn have a beautiful view of Fairy Lake where an occasional blue heron rises majestically from the shores. Many of the lodgings are in individual cottages along the lake front—a very pleasant place for a holiday in any season of the year.

2 cups broccoli (fresh or frozen) uncooked, finely chopped
1 small onion, finely chopped
3 cups chicken or turkey stock
1 cup potato water (reserved from cooking potatoes)
2 cups milk or cream
salt
pepper
seasoned salt
3 oz. crumbled blue cheese
paprika or 1 tsp. parsley (chopped)

In a 3-quart stockpot cook broccoli and onion in stock and potato water. (If you prefer firmer broccoli, do not overcook.) Add milk and let simmer, being careful not to let it boil. Season to taste with salt and pepper, adding additional spices, if desired. Add blue cheese just before serving, allowing it to melt. Serve with a dash of paprika or a sprinkle of chopped parsley. Serves 6.

MEATBALL SOUP

BLACK POINT INN, Prouts Neck, Maine
The great American artist and illustrator Winslow Homer made Prouts Neck his home for many years, and some of his most famous paintings and drawings were done at his studio which is just a few steps from this luxurious resort inn. It has been popular as a summer resort since the end of the 19th century.

3/4 lb. lean ground beef
1/4 lb. lean ground pork
1/4 cup bread crumbs
1/2 cup grated Parmesan cheese
1 tbsp. chopped parsley
1 clove garlic, minced
1/2 cup milk
2 eggs, beaten
1 1/2 tsp. salt
1/4 tsp. coarsely ground black pepper
1 qt. chicken broth
1 lb. escarole
1 cup of uncooked small pasta

Combine all ingredients except chicken broth and escarole. Shape them into 1" diameter meatballs. Heat the chicken broth and cook the escarole 20 minutes. Add the meatballs and simmer 10 minutes. Meanwhile, cook pasta in boiling water until just tender. Drain and add to soup. Serves 8 to 10.

NORTH HERO HOUSE

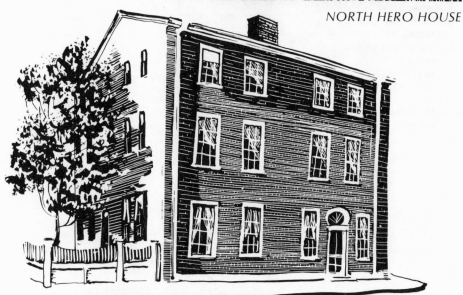

WINDSOR HOUSE

THE OBAN INN

CHABLIS CHEDDAR CHEESE SOUP

NORTH HERO HOUSE, North Hero, Vermont
This is a wonderful place for families, with endless activities for both children and adults—boating, water skiing, snorkeling, fishing, tennis, bicycling, horseback riding—or just enjoying Lake Champlain.

2 tbsp. butter
1/2 cup finely chopped
  celery
1 cup vertically very thinly
  sliced onion
2 10 3/4-oz. cans chicken
  broth
2 cups milk
1 tbsp. cornstarch
1/4 tsp. paprika
pinch freshly grated
  nutmeg
2 cups grated yellow
  cheddar cheese
1/2 cup Chablis wine
1 cup heavy cream
salt
freshly ground black
  pepper
croutons for garnish

In a 3-quart saucepan, melt butter and sauté celery and onions until onions are translucent. Pour in chicken broth and milk, and stir in cornstarch, 1/4 teaspoon paprika, and nutmeg. Bring to a boil, then reduce to medium heat. Add cheese. When cheese has melted, add wine and cream. Season to taste with salt and pepper and simmer, stirring occasionally, until soup is heated through. To serve, sprinkle the soup with paprika and garnish with croutons. Serves 6.

TOMATO SOUP

WINDSOR HOUSE, Newburyport, Massachusetts
Not just any tomato soup, but a special tomato soup prepared by Chef Fritz Crumb in his own kitchen at this unique North Shore inn. I hope mine tastes as good as his. Newburyport is an exceptionally well-preserved old New England town.

1 tbsp. butter
2 tsp. Shaker Herbal
  Bouquet*
1 1-lb. can plum tomatoes,
  drained
1 cup chicken stock
2 cups half-&-half
salt to taste
dash Tabasco

Available from The Society of Shakers. A similar mixture would be a combination of 6 parts parsley to 1 part basil, marjoram, oregano, summer savory, tarragon, thyme, and 1/2 part sage.

In a 3-quart saucepan, melt the butter. Add Herbal Bouquet; stir over medium heat 2 minutes. Add tomatoes, crushing them with a wooden spoon. Cook until soft. Rub tomato mixture through a sieve or food mill, discarding all remaining solids. Return tomato mixture to saucepan. Add chicken stock, half-&-half, salt to taste and Tabasco. Stirring constantly, heat the soup but do not boil. Allow the soup to stand 2 hours at room temperature or overnight in the refrigerator. Reheat before serving. Serves 6.

MONGOL SOUP

THE OBAN INN, Niagara on the Lake, Ontario, Canada
Because of its evident English heritage, this inn reminds me of other inns that I have visited, including the Crown at Chiddingfold and the Mermaid Tavern in Rye. It offers a substantial bar lunch and also serves a delicious afternoon tea. Niagara on the Lake is the home of the Shaw Drama Festival.

· **Navy Bean Soup (below)**
Lentil Soup (below)
2 qts. cream
curry

Combine the two soups, adding the cream and curry to taste. Serves 12 to 16.

NAVY BEAN SOUP:

2 quarts water
6 cups beans
1 cup diced carrots
1 cup diced celery
1 cup diced onions
1 large ham bone or cut up ham
salt and pepper to taste

In a large stockpot, soak beans overnight. Add remaining ingredients and bring to boil; simmer for 2 to 3 hours. Serves 6 to 8.

LENTIL SOUP:

2 quarts water
6 cups lentils
1 1/2 cups diced carrots
1 1/2 cups diced onions
1 1/2 cups diced celery
1 1/2 cups mashed potatoes
1 ham bone
1 1/2 cups chicken stock
salt and pepper to taste

In a large stockpot bring all ingredients to boil; simmer for 3 hours. Serves 6 to 8.

SALADS

HOMEWOOD INN

HOUND EARS LODGE

THE ALBEMARLE HOTEL

MOLDED CRABMEAT SALAD

HOMEWOOD INN, Yarmouth, Maine

Nestled on the shores of Casco Bay on Maine's rocky northern coast, the Home-wood has been a center of hospitality since the early 1930s. Among stands of juniper, maples, and Norway pines, accommodations are in snug cabins, many with a view of the water. The Webster family graciously agreed to share this succulent recipe.

1 1/2 cups cooked
   crabmeat
3/4 cup finely diced celery
1 pimiento, chopped
1 1/2 tsp. grated onion
12 stuffed olives, sliced
1 cup cooked peas
juice of 1 lemon
1 tsp. Worcestershire sauce
salt
freshly ground black
   pepper
1 1/2 tbsp. gelatin softened
   in 5 tbsp. water
1 cup mayonnaise

In a large bowl, combine crabmeat, celery, pimiento, onion, olives, and peas. Sprinkle with lemon juice, Worcestershire, and salt and pepper to taste.

Dissolve the softened gelatin over hot water and cool. Before gelatin congeals, add mayonnaise and mix. Pour gelatin mixture over crabmeat ingredients and combine quickly and thoroughly. Transfer to an oiled 1-quart ring mold and chill. Serves 6.

SHRIMP SALAD

HOUND EARS LODGE, Blowing Rock, North Carolina

Here is a luxurious American plan resort-inn in the northern mountains of the Tarheel State. In the summertime it provides championship golf, tennis, and startling scenery. In the winter, the emphasis is on downhill skiing. Any visitor should prepare to be enchanted.

1 lb. green, peeled,
   deveined, and cooked
   shrimp, chopped
2 hard-cooked eggs,
   chopped
1 stalk celery, chopped
2 tbsp. green relish
   (or substitute sweet
    pickles, chopped)
1 tbsp. capers
2 tbsp. lemon juice
1 tbsp. Worcestershire
   sauce
1 cup mayonnaise
1/2 tsp. salt
pinch freshly ground black
   pepper

In a large mixing bowl, combine all ingredients. Chill. Serves 4.

COLD SPAGHETTI SALAD

INN ON THE COMMON, Craftsbury Common, Vermont

Penny and Michael Schmidt are the hosts at this inn on the edge of Vermont's Northern Kingdom. It's a place for cross-country skiing in the winter, and walking in the wonderful countryside, as well as swimming, boating, and tennis in the summer. Penny says this is a showy dish with nice blendings of color and flavor—their guests seem to love it.

1/2 cup wine vinegar
3 tsp. Dijon-type mustard
5 cloves garlic, mashed
2 cups olive oil
1/2 lb. vermicelli
1 14 oz. can artichoke
hearts, quartered
1/2 lb. fresh mushrooms,
thinly sliced
1 large avocado, thinly
sliced
3 large tomatoes, coarsely
chopped

In a small mixing bowl, combine vinegar, mustard, garlic, and olive oil. Cook vermicelli according to directions on package, being careful not to overcook. Immediately after draining pasta, transfer it to a serving bowl and mix thoroughly with 2/3 of the oil and vinegar mixture. Marinate 3 to 4 hours in refrigerator, tossing occasionally to keep vermicelli coated. In the remaining oil and vinegar mixture, marinate artichokes, mushrooms and avocado. To serve, combine all ingredients and toss well. Serves 6.

MIREILLE'S SALADE VINAIGRETTE

PROSPECT HILL, Trevilians, Virginia

One of thirteen plantations designated as a National Historic District, Prospect Hill is one of the oldest homes in this area of Virginia. Today, it is being restored by innkeepers Bill and Mireille Sheehan, who offer their guests such niceties as breakfast in bed, homemade breads, and menus with a French accent.

3 or 4 heads leaf lettuce
(or Boston)
2 large cloves garlic,
minced
1/2 tsp. salt
1/4 cup olive oil
1/4 cup vegetable oil
1/4 cup wine vinegar
1 tsp. dried crumbled basil
(or 2 tbsp. fresh)
1 egg
Tomato wedges for garnish

Wash and pat dry lettuce. Mash garlic with salt to form a paste. In large bowl combine garlic paste, oils, and vinegar. Whisk to blend well. Allow to stand 10 minutes or longer. To serve, add basil and raw egg, and whisk again. Pour over lettuce, toss well, garnish with tomato wedges. Serves 12.

INN ON THE COMMON

PROSPECT HILL

COLBY HILL INN

THE BRIARS

EAGLES MERE INN

PATCHWORK QUILT

CAULIFLOWER AND MUSHROOM SALAD

THE BRIARS, Jackson Point, Ontario, Canada

This spacious resort-inn is on 200 acres of land which has belonged to the Sibbald family for over a century. Innkeeper John Sibbald's great-great-grandmother came to this part of Ontario in 1835. Now the house and seventeen guest cottages provide lodgings for guests who can swim, golf, play tennis, or any of a dozen other things year-round.

1 fresh cauliflower
1/2 lb. fresh mushrooms,
   thickly sliced
3 green onions, thinly
   sliced
1 tbsp. diced pimiento
1 tsp. chopped parsley
1 cup Chef's Special
   Dressing (below)
Boston lettuce

Cut cauliflower in small rosettes, blanch 1 min. in boiling water with touch of vinegar. Cool. Combine with remaining ingredients, marinate 1 hour. Drain and reserve the sauce. Set the salad over Boston lettuce. Pour sauce over just before serving. Serves 8.

CHEF'S SPECIAL DRESSING:

1/3 cup cider vinegar
1 tsp. salt
1 tsp. dry mustard
2 tsp. sugar
1/2 tsp. pepper
2 cloves garlic, crushed
Juice of 1 lemon
2 cups vegetable oil

Combine all ingredients, except vegetable oil. Allow to stand 10 minutes. Add oil, shake well. Yield: 2 1/2 cups dressing.

MUSTARD RING

EAGLES MERE INN, Eagles Mere, Pennsylvania

A 2,000-foot-high lake and surrounding mountains provide many diversions for this warm-hearted, family-run inn in the Alleghenies, about an hour's drive north of Williamsport.

1/2 cup cider vinegar
1/2 cup water
3/4 cup sugar
3 tbsp. dry mustard
1/2 tsp. turmeric
salt
4 eggs, beaten
1 tbsp. gelatin softened in
   1/2 cup water
1 cup heavy cream,
   whipped
cherry tomatoes for garnish
watercress sprigs for garnish

In the top of a double boiler, combine vinegar, water, sugar, dry mustard, turmeric, and salt to taste. Add eggs. Cook the mixture until thick; then stir in softened gelatin. Cool. When mixture is cool, fold in whipped cream and pour into a 1-quart ring mold. Chill until firm. Unmold and garnish center and circumference of mustard ring with cherry tomatoes and watercress sprigs. Do not use lettuce. Mustard ring is delicious with baked ham. Serves 8.

BLUE CHEESE DRESSING

COLBY HILL INN, Henniker, New Hampshire
Many country antiques decorate this trim little inn which was built in 1821. The dining room with its pewter serving plates and gay linen is a popular meeting place where guests enjoy the friendly atmosphere and good food.

1 1/2 cups olive oil
2/3 cup red wine vinegar
4 tbsp. New Hampshire
   maple syrup
2 garlic cloves, crushed
1 tsp. dry mustard
2 tsp. paprika
1/4 tsp. salt
1/4 tsp. freshly ground
   black pepper
6 oz. blue cheese,
   crumbled

At high speed, blend for 2 minutes all the ingredients except the blue cheese. Then add the cheese and combine thoroughly. Cover and refrigerate until ready to use. Yield: 3 cups dressing.

COUNTRY HOUSE DRESSING

PATCHWORK QUILT, Middlebury, Indiana
Milton and Arletta Lovejoy, along with Herb and Treva Swarm, have lovingly preserved the atmosphere of a real farm for many years at this restaurant in Northern Indiana. I visited it for the first time in 1970, and on each subsequent visit I find new innovations and dishes to tempt me even further.

2 qts. mayonnaise
6 cups chili sauce
1/2 cup chopped green
   onions
1/2 cup sweet pickle relish
8 hard-cooked eggs, finely
   chopped
2 tsp. salt
1 tsp. freshly ground
   black pepper
1/4 cup Worcestershire
   sauce
dash Tabasco
1/2 cup chopped stuffed
   olives

Combine all ingredients. Refrigerate in a covered container. Serve chilled. Yield: 1 gallon dressing.

THE SAUCE

COBB'S COVE, Barnstable Village, Massachusetts
The Keeping Room's Count Rumford fireplace in this beautiful colonial-style salt-box manor provides a cozy, warm gathering-place where guests can enjoy lively conversations about their adventures on the nearby beaches, or in and around this Cape Cod village's fascinating craft shops. While this recipe is in our salad section, be sure to try it on vegetables—I had it on hot broccoli, and it was wonderful!

1 large head garlic
2 1/2 cups wine vinegar
6 tbsp. salt
2 tbsp. freshly ground
 black pepper
5 cups olive oil

Peel all garlic cloves. In a blender or food processor, combine garlic, vinegar, salt and pepper; blend several minutes. Transfer to a half-gallon plastic container with a screw-on lid. Add olive oil. Shake container vigorously prior to pouring. Yield: Approximately 7 cups sauce.

This sauce enhances both hot and cold foods; it is tasty on artichokes, broccoli, green beans, and asparagus. Also excellent on green salads as well as chef's salads.

HOUSE DRESSING

THE ALBEMARLE HOTEL, St. Petersburg, Florida
There's never a dull moment here, with some sort of planned entertainment going on all the time, whether it's a cruise on Tampa Bay, a trip to Cypress Gardens, a game of shuffleboard, or watching one of the major baseball teams in training. At the same time it's rather homey, with a menu featuring such hearty fare as Yankee pot roast, roast loin of pork, and lamb shanks.

1 11 oz. can tomato soup
1/2 cup vinegar
1 tsp. dry mustard
1 tsp. paprika
2 tsp. salt
2 tbsp. grated onion
1 cup vegetable oil
pinch sugar
1 tsp. Worcestershire
 sauce

Combine all ingredients in a 1-quart lidded jar and refrigerate. Before using, shake well. Good with avocado, tomato, and lettuce salad. Yield: Approximately 3 cups dressing.

CLASSIC ORIENTAL DRESSING

1770 HOUSE, East Hampton, New York

Meals at this beautiful old house tend to be unusual and elegant, as chef Miriam Perle is a Cordon Bleu cook and was head of a cooking school for twelve years. Her cuisine is eclectic, ranging from country lentil soup to steamed sole Chinois. She uses this dressing on her Oriental Crabmeat Salad.

1 egg
3/4 cup vegetable oil
1/4 cup Chinese sesame
  oil
2 tbsp. soy sauce
2 tbsp. Dijon-type mustard
1 tsp. sugar
1 tbsp. wine vinegar
2 garlic cloves, minced
1 tsp. peeled, minced
  ginger root
1 tsp. lemon juice
salt to taste
freshly ground black
  pepper to taste

In a blender or food processor, beat egg until thick and light colored. Slowly add oils, then remaining ingredients. Check seasoning and adjust if necessary. Yield: 1 1/2 cup dressing. This is wonderful on cold chicken or noodles, crabmeat or shrimp salad.

POPPY SEED DRESSING

THE SQUIRE TARBOX INN, Westport Island, Maine

An air of relaxed, quiet enjoyment is the hallmark of this beautiful old house, built in 1763. Innkeepers Anne McInvale and Elsie White offer their guests a slice of New England country life with such pursuits as berrying, walking in the woodlands, or playing darts in the barn. Vegetables come from their own garden.

1 1/2 cups sugar
2 tsp. dry mustard
2 tsp. salt
2/3 cup vinegar
3 tbsp. onion juice
2 cups vegetable oil
3 tbsp. poppy seeds

Mix sugar, mustard, salt, and vinegar. Add onion juice and stir thoroughly. Add oil slowly, beating constantly until thick. Add poppy seeds and beat for a few minutes. Store in refrigerator, but not near the freezing coil. Yield: 3 1/2 cups. This dressing is delicious on fruit salads.

FISH

AND SHELLFISH

THE FARMHOUSE

TANQUE VERDE

THE SILVERMINE TAVERN

SALMON MISOYAKI

THE FARMHOUSE, Port Townsend, Washington
The Farmhouse is a genuine gourmet restaurant with different types of cuisine featured each month, including Hungarian, northern Chinese, Italian, German, and Japanese. There are no overnight accommodations, but people in the Seattle area are happy to drive many miles to savour John Ashby Conway's truly unusual offerings. One of his guests, a chef himself, after eating this dish said, "I've been cooking fish all my life—this is the best I've ever eaten!"

4 lbs. salmon (or ling cod) fillets
3/4 cup, plus 1/2 tsp., Kikkoman soy sauce
1/4 cup sherry
2 cloves garlic, thinly sliced
4 slices fresh ginger root (size of a quarter)
2 tbsp. sugar
1/4 cup shiromiso (white miso)*

Place fish in shallow pan. In a small bowl combine the 3/4 cup of soy sauce, sherry, garlic, and ginger; pour over fish. Marinate for 1/2 hour, turning the fish in the marinade. Preheat oven 350° to 400° (depending on thickness and moisture of fish). Thin the miso with the 1/2 tsp. of soy sauce and spread this mixture over the fish. Bake in upper third of oven for 20 to 25 minutes, or until fish flakes when prodded gently with a fork or a milky substance begins to exude. Serve with either of following sauces. Serves 6 to 8.

SAUCE AIOLI:

1 head garlic
2 cups packed fresh parsley
1 tbsp. dried oregano or basil leaves
2 or 3 tbsps. olive or salad oil
2 cups mayonnaise, to taste

Make a pesto, using blender or processor, with all the ingredients except the mayonnaise. When the paste is thoroughly blended, add mayonnaise to taste. Yield: 2 1/2 cups. This sauce keeps well in the refrigerator and can be used with added salt as a dressing for a roast of beef before it goes into the oven. It is excellent with green vegetables or cauliflower.

JAPANESE SAUCE:

1 part Kikkoman soy sauce
10 parts mayonnaise

Mix ingredients together well. This is excellent also on artichokes, broccoli, tomatoes, and cold beans.

*Obtainable at Japanese grocers. It keeps almost indefinitely in the refrigerator. Try some in vegetable or cream soups!

CABRILLA (RED SNAPPER)

TANQUE VERDE, Tucson, Arizona

Tanque Verde is a guest ranch with a history dating back to the days when the Apaches were on the warpath. Today guests enjoy trail riding in the high desert country and real ranch-hand meals. Tanque Verde serves this dish with sautéed cherry tomatoes.

4 6-8 oz. cabrilla or red
   snapper fillets
olive oil
salt
white pepper
4 tbsp. water
1 1/2 cups Avocado Sauce
   (below)
12 avocado slices
sliced ripe olives for
   garnish

Prepare Avocado Sauce. Preheat oven to 350°. Place fillets in a single layer in shallow baking pan, brush with olive oil. Sprinkle with salt and pepper. Add 4 tablespoons of water. Bake uncovered for 20 minutes or until fish flakes easily when prodded with fork. Remove from oven and drain off water. Cover each fillet with Avocado Sauce. Top each fillet with 3 slices of avocado and sliced olives. Return to oven for about 6 minutes. Serves 4.

AVOCADO SAUCE:

Pulp of 2 large, ripe
   avocadoes
2 tbsp. lime juice
2 canned green chilis
   rinsed, seeded, and
   chopped
1 tbsp. chopped fresh
   coriander (or 1/2 tsp.
   ground coriander)
1 clove garlic, finely
   minced
salt
2 large ripe tomatoes,
   seeded, juiced, and
   diced

In blender mash avocado pulp with lime juice. Add green chilis to blender, and continue to blend. Add coriander and garlic and salt to taste. Add but do not blend diced tomatoes. Drain. Yield: 1 1/2 cups.

OYSTERS VICTORIA

THE SILVERMINE TAVERN, Norwalk, Connecticut

This cozy inn hidden away in the Norwalk woods about an hour from New York City has its own millpond with ducks and geese. In winter, lunch and dinner is frequently served to the accompaniment of a crackling fire in the fireplace.

3 cups baby shrimp,
   cooked and peeled
3 cups fresh shucked
   oysters, with their liquor
4 cups Mornay Sauce
   (below)

Preheat oven to 350°. Prepare Mornay Sauce. Line bottom of a small, shallow buttered baking dish with the shrimp. Cover the shrimp with a layer of oysters. Cover with Mornay Sauce. Bake 20 minutes. Do not overcook as the oysters will become tough. Brown under the broiler if desired. Serves 4.

MORNAY SAUCE:

6 tbsp. butter
6 tbsp. flour
3 cups light cream
1 cup grated cheddar
1/2 cup grated Parmesan
  cheese

Melt butter in saucepan, add flour and simmer 3 minutes. Add cream and stir until thickened. Slowly add cheese until all is melted and sauce is smooth. Yield: 4 cups.

CIOPPINO

THE RED LION INN, Stockbridge, Massachusetts
For many guests, the Red Lion is a first country inn experience. They are usually impressed with the low-ceilinged lobby with its ancient grandfather clock, cheery fireplace, and collection of pitchers. Stockbridge is the home of the Norman Rockwell Museum, the Berkshire Theater Festival, and the Tanglewood Music Festival. Nearby backroading is exceptional.

3 tbsp. olive oil
1 cup onion, coarsely
  chopped
1 cup green pepper,
  coarsely chopped
1 tbsp. crushed garlic
2 cups fish stock or canned
  clam juice
1 cup fresh tomatoes,
  coarsely chopped
1/2 cup dry white wine
2 tbsp. fresh parsley, finely
  chopped
1 bay leaf
salt
pepper
4 soft-shell crabs or
  Dungeness crab (4-8)
  pieces
8-12 mussels in the shell
8-12 clams in the shell
4-8 large shrimp, shelled
12 oz. cod, halibut, sea-
  bass or any combination
  of firm- fleshed white
  fish, cubed
dry sherry

In a 2- or 3-quart enameled or stainless steel pot heat the olive oil over moderate heat until a light haze forms. Add onions, green pepper, and garlic. Cook for 5 minutes stirring frequently or until onions are soft and translucent but not brown. Stir in fish stock or clam juice, tomatoes, wine, parsley, and bay leaf. Bring to boil, reduce heat, and simmer partially covered for 30 minutes, then add salt and pepper to taste.

To assemble Cioppino, arrange soft-shell or Dungeness crabs in the bottom of a 3- to 5-quart lidded casserole or skillet. Lay mussels, clams, and shrimp on the top and pour in the tomato mixture. Bring to a boil, reduce heat to low, cover tightly and cook for 10 minutes. Add fish, cover casserole again and cook for another 5 to 10 minutes. The Cioppino is done when the mussel and clam shells have opened and fish flakes easily when prodded gently with a fork. Discard any mussels or clams that remain closed. Serve at once directly from casserole, or spoon the fish and shellfish into a large heated tureen and pour the tomato mixture over them. Add a dash of sherry to Cioppino before serving. Serves 4.

BAKED FLOUNDER WITH SCALLOP STUFFING

LARCHWOOD INN, Wakefield, Rhode Island

Rhode Island has some of the most enjoyable beaches in the northeast. Fortunately, flounder and scallops abound, and this dish is one of those most frequently ordered at this former mansion.

SCALLOP STUFFING:

1/2 cup butter
1 clove garlic, minced
1 small onion, finely chopped
1/2 lb. scallops, chopped
salt
freshly ground black pepper
dry white wine
fine bread crumbs

In a 10" skillet, melt the 1/2 cup butter. Add garlic and onion and saute until onions are translucent. Add scallops and cook 2 or 3 minutes. Season with salt, pepper, and white wine to taste. Add sufficient bread crumbs to prepare a moist stuffing.

6 5-7 oz. flounder fillets (2-2 1/2 lbs.)
1/4 cup butter, melted
1/2 cup hot water

Place each flounder fillet dark side up on a flat surface. Placing the scallop stuffing in the center of each fillet, divide evenly among the fillets. Fold both ends of each fillet over the stuffing, overlapping the ends. Pour melted butter and the hot water into a 9x12" baking dish. Transfer the stuffed fillets to the baking dish and bake 20 minutes while you prepare a white sauce.

WHITE SAUCE:

2 tbsp. butter
2 tbsp. flour
1 cup milk
salt
freshly ground black pepper
dry white wine

In a small saucepan, melt butter, then whisk in flour. Cook over low heat 2 to 3 minutes, whisking constantly. Then add milk, and salt, pepper and white wine to taste. Increase heat to medium, whisking constantly until the sauce is thickened. Cook several minutes over low heat, stirring.

When the flounder has baked 20 minutes, pour the white sauce over the stuffed fillets. Return the baking dish to the oven briefly and heat until the sauce begins to bubble. Serves 6.

LARCHWOOD INN

THE RED LION INN

MILFORD HOUSE

LOBSTER AU GRATIN

KILMUIR PLACE, Northeast Margaree, Nova Scotia, Canada
Innkeeper Isabel Taylor boasts that she's never used a mix in her life, and never will at this tiny guest house which is located on the famous Cabot Trail at the far end of Nova Scotia. Many are the times I have sat in her kitchen and savored the magic aromas of roast beef, lobster, and chocolate cake. This is one of Isabel's most sought-after recipes.

5 tbsp. butter
2 tbsp. flour
1 1/2 cup light cream
1/2 tsp. dry mustard
3 tbsp. grated Parmesan
  cheese
salt
freshly ground black
  pepper
1 egg yolk, slightly beaten
1 lb. cooked lobster meat,
  chopped
1/2 cup sliced, sautéed
  mushrooms
2 tbsp. dry sherry

Preheat oven to 400°. In a saucepan, prepare the cream sauce: Melt two tablespoons of the butter, add flour, stirring constantly. When flour and butter are blended, gradually pour in cream. Add mustard and 2 tablespoons of the cheese. Simmer, stirring until sauce is thick and smooth. Season to taste with salt and pepper. Stir a small portion of sauce into the egg yolk and add to remaining contents of saucepan. Gradually add one tablespoon of the butter, lobster and sautéed mushrooms. Stir in sherry. Transfer to a 2-quart ovenproof casserole. Sprinkle with the remaining tablespoon of cheese. Dot with the remaining two tablespoons of butter. Bake 15 minutes. Serves 4.

SCALLOP CASSEROLE

MILFORD HOUSE, South Milford, Nova Scotia, Canada
With 24 cabins nestled in a woodland setting surrounding two lakes, this rustic resort-inn offers no end of possibilities for fun and sports, rest and relaxation. When a guest leaves, everyone remaining stands on the porch and waves until the departing guest passes the oak tree at the corner.

1 lb. bay scallops
salt, plus 1 tsp. salt for
  white sauce
2 tbsp. butter, plus 7 tbsp.
  butter, melted
1 1/2 cup diced celery
1/2 cup minced onion
1 cup sliced mushrooms
1/4 cup flour
2 cups milk
1 cup bread crumbs
1/2 cup grated cheese

Preheat oven to 375°. Grease an 8" baking pan. Spread scallops on plate and sprinkle with salt. In a medium-sized skillet melt the 2 tablespoons of butter and add vegetables. Cook over low heat until vegetables are limp but not brown. Set aside. In a 3-quart saucepan, over medium heat, combine 4 tablespoons of the melted butter with flour. Gradually add milk, whisking constantly until sauce is thickened and smooth. Add cooked vegetables and scallops. Transfer to prepared baking pan. Top with bread crumbs, grated cheese, and remaining 3 tablespoons of melted butter. Bake 20 minutes. Serves 6.

CRABMEAT SNUG HARBOR

WHISTLING OYSTER RESTAURANT, Ogunquit, Maine
This superb and delightful restaurant is right on the waters of the sheltered harbor of Perkins Cove. The ambience and the scenery make a visit here even more than a gastronomic event. Crabmeat Snug Harbor has been one of my favorites ever since my first visit there in 1969.

1 1/2 cups heavy cream
1/2 cup fish broth or
  bottled clam juice
1 tbsp. Worcestershire
  sauce
pinch freshly grated
  nutmeg
1 tsp. dry mustard
2 tsp. paprika
1/2 bay leaf
salt
white pepper
2 tbsp. butter
3 tbsp. flour
1/4 cup dry sherry
1 lb. cooked fresh
  crabmeat
4 tbsp. grated sharp white
  cheddar cheese

Preheat oven to 350°. In a 3-quart saucepan, combine heavy cream, fish broth or clam juice, Worcestershire, nutmeg, dry mustard, paprika, bay leaf, salt and white pepper to taste. Over medium flame, heat through but do not allow to boil. In another 3-quart saucepan, melt butter then whisk in flour. Cook over low heat several minutes, then, stirring constantly, slowly add seasoned cream. Bring to boil; reduce heat and simmer 5 to 10 minutes. Add dry sherry and set aside to cool slightly. Taste for seasoning.

In one large ovenproof casserole or four individual baking dishes or seafood shells, layer sauce and crabmeat, beginning and finishing with sauce. Sprinkle with grated cheese and bake until bubbly and golden brown. Serves 4.

DEVILED SCALLOPS

SHAW'S HOTEL, Brackley Beach, Prince Edward Island, Canada
In the same family since 1860, this country hotel has been entertaining guests with summer activities ranging from horseback riding to deep sea fishing for many years.

2 cloves garlic, crushed
2 tbsp. butter, melted
2 tbsp. flour
1/2 tsp. dry mustard
2 tsp. grated horseradish
1/2 tsp. celery salt
freshly ground black
  pepper
2 tbsp. chopped parsley
1 tbsp. lemon juice
1 lb. scallops
1/2 cup buttered cracker
  crumbs
paprika

Preheat oven to 350°. Butter four scallop shells. In a large saucepan, sauté garlic in melted butter. Add flour and all seasonings to contents of saucepan. Stir in scallops and cook 4 to 5 minutes. Divide scallop mixture among the prepared shells. Top with buttered crumbs and paprika. Bake 20 minutes. Serves 4.

SCALLOPS FRANCOISE

DEXTER'S INN, Sunapee, New Hampshire

In winter the guests at Dexter's enjoy cross-country skiing on the grounds, and in summer they return for some lively tennis. In all seasons, Frank Simpson says this is a nice change from the usual broiled-in butter scallops.

1 lb. bay scallops or sea
   scallops cut into bite-
   size pieces
1 cup water
1/2 cup dry white wine
3 tbsp. butter, plus 2 tbsp.
   butter, melted
3 tbsp. flour
1/2 tsp. salt
1/4 tsp. paprika
1 egg yolk, beaten
1/4 cup shredded natural
   cheddar cheese
1 tbsp. pimiento (optional)
1 cup soft bread crumbs

Preheat oven to 400°. In a 2-quart sauce-pan, boil the scallops in the water and white wine for 2 minutes or until scallops begin to shrink. Drain, reserving the liquid. In a 3- to 4-quart saucepan, melt 3 table-spoons of the butter, stir in the flour, salt, and paprika and, whisking constantly, pour in the reserved scallop liquid. Cook over low heat until the sauce is thick and bubbly. Gradually blend in the egg yolk, cheese, (and pimiento, if you are using it). Add the scallops and cook over low heat until the cheese has melted. Transfer the creamed scallops to four 6-inch ramekins or scallop shells. In a small bowl combine the bread crumbs and the two tablespoons of melted butter and sprinkle the crumbs over the scallops. Bake 5 minutes or until sauce begins to bubble and bread crumbs are golden. Serves 4.

FILLET OF SOLE

BIRD AND BOTTLE, Garrison, New York

Amenities are always special here—snowy linen and sparkling glasses in the dining room; four cozy and beautifully furnished bedrooms with woodburning fireplaces—and the food is nonpareil.

3/4 cup dry white wine
finely chopped shallots
6 5- to 6-oz. fillets of sole
2 large tomatoes, peeled,
   seeded, and minced
1 cup sliced fresh
   mushrooms
1 1/2 cups fish stock

SAUCE:

2 egg yolks
1/2 cup butter, melted,
   plus 1/4 cup butter

Preheat oven to 350°. Place wine and shallots in a large ovenproof sauté pan. Cook over low heat until wine is reduced to 1 tablespoon. Arrange fish over shallots. Cover with tomatoes, mushrooms, and fish stock. Cover the sauté pan and bake 15 minutes or until fish flakes easily when lightly prodded with a fork. Remove from oven; drain and discard stock. Meanwhile, make sauce.

Preheat broiler. In a medium-sized mixing bowl, beat egg yolks until thickened, then gradually beat in the 1/2 cup melted butter. In a small saucepan, melt the remaining

2 tbsp. flour
1 cup milk, scalded
1/4 tsp. white pepper
Dash of nutmeg
1 cup heavy cream,
  whipped

1/4 cup butter. Gradually whisk in the flour, stirring constantly until flour and butter are well blended. Add scalded milk. Cook over medium heat, stirring, until thickened. Cool. Whisk in egg yolk mixture; add white pepper and nutmeg.

Fold whipped cream into sauce and spoon over fish. Broil until golden brown. Serves 6.

FILLET OF SOLE STUFFED WITH SALMON MOUSSE

VICTORIAN INN, Whitinsville, Massachusetts
There is a sense of graciousness and comfort in the spacious rooms of this imposing mansion. I am particularly partial to the book-lined dining room where gourmet dishes like this one are served.

SALMON MOUSSE FILLING:

1/2 cup (4 oz.) cream
  cheese, softened
1 egg
lemon juice
salt
pepper
1 7-oz. cooked, flaked
  salmon steak or 1 7-oz.
  can cooked salmon,
  flaked

In a medium-sized bowl, combine cream cheese, egg, lemon juice, salt and pepper to taste. Add salmon and blend thoroughly. The mixture must be stiff. Refrigerate to stiffen it. While salmon mixture is chilling, prepare sauce.

SAUCE:

3/4 cup clam juice
1/2 cup milk
4 tbsp. butter
4 tbsp. flour
1/2 cup heavy cream
2 tbsp. lemon juice
1 tbsp. crumbled dried
  tarragon
salt
pepper

In a saucepan bring clam juice and milk to a boil. Meanwhile, in another saucepan, melt butter, then add flour, whisking constantly. Gradually add hot clam juice mixture, whisking. When the sauce is smooth and thick, add heavy cream, lemon juice, tarragon, salt and pepper to taste, and stir until thoroughly blended.

FILLET OF SOLE:

4 8-oz. fillets of sole
1/2 cup grated Swiss
  cheese

Preheat oven to 350°. Pour some of the sauce into the bottom of a 9x13″ baking dish. Depending on size of fillet, use 2 to 4 tablespoons of salmon mousse to each fillet and wrap the fillet around a cylinder of mousse. Place stuffed sole in baking pan and cover with remaining sauce. Sprinkle with grated cheese and bake 20 to 30 minutes, or until sauce is bubbly. Serves 4.

OYSTER PIE

STAGECOACH INN, Sheffield, Massachusetts

"An English inn in the Berkshires" is one way to describe this beautiful red brick building which is set at the foot of the mountains in the south Berkshires. Just to make it more fun, innkeeper John Pedretti is from Italy and his wife Ann is from England. Both the inn and the setting remind me of a similar hostelry in northern Yorkshire.

1/2 cup dry white wine
1/2 cup water
12 tbsp. (3/4 cup) butter
1 small onion
1 bay leaf
1/2 gallon oysters, shucked, rinsed, and drained
8 tbsp. (1/2 cup) flour
salt
pepper
3 tbsp. finely chopped shallots
1 cup dry sherry
1 cup heavy cream
1/2 lb. mushrooms, sliced
pastry for a two-crust pie, see Pies

Preheat oven to 425°. In a 3-quart saucepan, bring to a boil the wine, water, 2 tablespoons of the butter, onion, and bay leaf. Add the oysters. When the oysters are tender and their edges begin to curl, remove them from the saucepan and strain, reserving the liquids.

Make a white sauce: In another 3-quart saucepan melt 8 tablespoons of the butter, then whisk in the flour and cook over low heat until the flour turns golden. Pour in the reserved oyster stock, season to taste with salt and pepper and cook over low heat, stirring constantly, until the sauce begins to thicken.

In another saucepan, melt the remaining 2 tablespoons of butter and sauté the shallots until they are translucent; then add the sherry and cook until the wine is almost completely reduced. Pour in the heavy cream and cook until the liquids are reduced by half. Stir into the white sauce. Check for seasoning.

To assemble the oyster pies: divide the oysters among 6 small oval pie dishes. Top with the mushrooms. Into each pie dish, pour sauce almost to fill each dish. Roll out the pastry dough and make a lid for each of the dishes. Bake until crust is golden brown, about 15 to 20 minutes. Serves 6.

COQUILLE OF SEAFOOD CARDINALE

THE BUXTON INN, Granville, Ohio

The origins of this Ohio hostelry have been traced back to 1812, and innkeepers Orville and Audrey Orr, as well as their staff, are dressed in the costumes of that period. Granville is the home of Denison University and the town was used as a setting for The Animal Kingdom, *a play written by James Thurber. Visitors to the inn, besides being impressed with the decor and menu, are always captivated by Major Buxton who is described by daughter Amy as "a very smart cat."*

SEAFOOD:

1 lb. bay scallops
1 lb. shrimp, peeled and
  deveined
1/2 lb. snow crabmeat
6 green onions, chopped
1/2 lb. mushrooms,
  chopped
1/4 cup clarified butter
salt
freshly ground black
  pepper
1/2 cup chopped pimiento

In a large saucepan, bring 3 quarts salted water to a boil. Cook the scallops and shrimp until they are tender. Strain and return liquid to saucepan and simmer for 1 1/2 hours until liquid is reduced to 1/4 cup. Reserve for use in the Cream Sauce. In a 10" skillet, sauté the onions and mushrooms in clarified butter. Season to taste with salt and pepper. Add the pimiento and set the mixture aside while you prepare the Cream Sauce.

CREAM SAUCE:

1 cup butter
1 tbsp. onion powder
1 tsp. garlic powder
1/4 tsp. white pepper
1/4 tsp. crumbled dried
  thyme
1/4 cup reserved seafood
  stock
1/4 cup dry sherry
1/2 cup flour
1 qt. half-&-half
1 pt. heavy cream
1 cup mayonnaise
4 tbsp. grated Parmesan
  cheese
1 tbsp. paprika

Melt butter in top of double boiler. Whisk in onion and garlic powders, white pepper, thyme, seafood stock, and sherry. Add flour and continue to whisk until a smooth paste is formed. Continue whisking as you add half-&-half and heavy cream. Cook over low heat 20 to 30 minutes. Yield: 1 1/2 quarts sauce.

In a large bowl, combine the seafood mixture, vegetables, and 1/2 the cream sauce, thoroughly coating the ingredients. Chill. Combine the remaining cream sauce and mayonnaise and chill.

To assemble Seafood Cardinale: Preheat oven to 400°. Divide chilled seafood mixture among 12 scallop shells. Cover with cream sauce and mayonnaise mixture. In a small bowl, combine Parmesan and paprika. Sprinkle over the contents of the shells. Bake 10 minutes or until Seafood Cardinale is browned and bubbly. Serves 6.

FISH BOIL

WHITE GULL, Fish Creek, Wisconsin
This is a scene of much friendly fun on the nights of the "fish boil" when guests sit outside, eat to their hearts' content, join in the singing, and generally have a good time. A Door County tradition since the 19th century, the fish boil was started by Scandinavian lumberjacks and fishermen.

NOTE: *This fish boil is traditionally prepared outside over a wood fire. If you use this method, when the fish is done, pour kerosene on the fire. When the fire flares, water will boil over carrying with it the fish oils. It may also be prepared on your home stove.*

16 small red potatoes
1 lb. salt for each 2 gallons water
16 fresh whitefish steaks (cut into 1"-thick cross sections; each serving of two steaks should weigh 1/2 to 3/4 lb.) or substitute trout, salmon or fish of similar size.

For flavor penetration, slice off a small portion of each potato. In a heavy pot large enough to hold the fish and potatoes, measure sufficient water to cover the potatoes. Bring water to a vigorous boil. Place potatoes in a net or wire basket, add to the boiling water and stir half the required amount of salt into the water. After 18 to 20 minutes potatoes should be almost tender. Add fish and remaining salt to the net or wire basket. Skimming fish oils continously, cook 7 to 8 minutes or until fish flakes easily when lightly prodded with a fork. Lift net or wire basket from pot and drain. Serve two potatoes and two fish steaks in each portion. Serves 8. Fish boil is traditionally accompanied by melted butter, coleslaw, rye bread, and cherry pie.

LEMON MUSHROOM SAUCE FOR FISH

MARATHON INN, Grand Manan Island, New Brunswick, Canada
This inn on an island off the New Brunswick coast, in the Bay of Fundy near the Calais, Maine, border-crossing, is a real adventure. The ferries run regularly and the prize is well worth the quest. Here is a sauce they serve on their wonderful fresh, baked fish.

1 10-oz. can mushroom pieces, including liquid
2 tbsp. chicken soup base
1 cup water
1/2 cup lemon juice
2 tbsp. butter
2 tbsp. flour combined with 2 tbsp. water

In a 2-quart saucepan, combine all ingredients except flour and water mixture and bring to a boil; thicken with flour and water and heat through. Yield: 3 cups sauce.

POULTRY
AND GAME

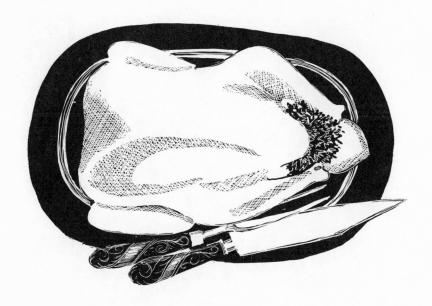

PINE BARN INN

GRISTMILL SQUARE

GRISWOLD INN

PENNSYLVANIA DUTCH-STYLE CHICKEN POT PIE

PINE BARN INN, Danville, Pennsylvania

Located in mid-Pennsylvania just off I-80 between the Ohio line and the Delaware Water Gap, the Pine Barn Inn in Danville is an ideal stop for anyone traversing the Keystone State. Barbara Walzer says of her husband-innkeeper: "Marty's waistline and age are running a race to see which one is going to reach forty first." It's a small wonder with dishes like this one.

2 1-lb stewing chickens
salt
pepper
1 small onion
leaves from 1 bunch celery

Season chickens with salt and pepper. Place them in a lidded pot large enough to hold the chickens comfortably. Add onion and celery leaves. Cover with water and boil. Cook until chicken is easily removed from the bones. Remove chicken, reserving broth. Strain the stock, return it to the covered pot and bring to a boil. Meanwhile, skin the chickens and remove the meat from the bones.

DOUGH:

4 cups flour
2 tsp. baking powder
1 tsp. salt
4 tbsp. shortening
4 eggs, beaten
2/3 cup ice water

In a large mixing bowl, combine flour, baking powder, salt, and shortening and crumble with your fingers until mixture has the consistency of coarse crumbs. Combine eggs and ice water and add to flour mixture, blending thoroughly. Using half of the dough at a time, roll it thin, incorporating additional flour if dough is sticky, then cut in 2-inch squares. Dry squares on a paper towel for 1 hour.

2 large peeled potatoes,
  thinly sliced
1 large onion, diced
1 onion, finely chopped
  (optional)

Into chicken broth place a layer of dough squares, then a layer of chicken, and finally a layer of potatoes and diced onions. Repeat this procedure until all components are used. Over medium heat and stirring occasionally, cook the pot pie, covered, 20 to 30 minutes or until the dough is done. Serve in bowls. Finely chopped raw onion may be served at the table as an optional garnish. This pot pie may be made with ham or beef. Serves 6.

SAUTÉED CHICKEN LIVERS IN PORT WINE SAUCE

GRISTMILL SQUARE, Warm Springs, Virginia
Cathy and Phillip Hirsh led the way in restoring this mountain village in the highlands of western Virginia in 1973. I happened by a few years later, and have been stopping regularly ever since. One of the many reasons is to enjoy these sautéed chicken livers which are served at the Water Wheel Restaurant.

PORT WINE SAUCE:

1 large shallot, chopped
2 tbsp. sliced mushrooms
2 tbsp. butter
3 tbsp. sour cream or yogurt
1/4 cup heavy cream
1/4 cup beef stock
1 tsp. paprika
1 tbsp. chopped parsley
1/4 cup Port wine

In a medium-sized skillet, sauté the shallot and mushrooms in butter until the shallot is soft. Add remaining ingredients and cook 2 to 3 minutes until sauce begins to bubble. Liquify in a blender and keep warm while you prepare the chicken livers. Yield: 1 cup sauce.

CHICKEN LIVERS:

1 lb. chicken livers, washed
2 tbsp. clarified butter
salt
freshly ground black pepper
8 toast points
parsley sprigs for garnish

In a 10 to 12″ skillet, sauté chicken livers in clarified butter until livers are 3/4 done. Pour Port Wine Sauce into the skillet and cook over low heat until the chicken livers are done. To serve, arrange two toast points per portion, pour the chicken livers and their sauce over the toast points and garnish with parsley sprigs. Serves 4.

MRS. GRISWOLD'S BREAST OF CHICKEN

GRISWOLD INN, Essex, Connecticut
Boats and boating and history are big in this old waterfront town. The Griswold is full of nearly three centuries of memorabilia, and there is literally no end of all kinds of things to see and do in this busy, lively place.

4 plump chicken breasts, boned (do not remove skins)
4 tbsps. butter
16 canned small artichoke hearts
2 cups sliced mushrooms
1/2 cup shallots, chopped
1/2 clove of garlic, slivered
1 cup dry white wine
1 tbsp. arrowroot or flour

Cut chicken breasts into small, bite-sized pieces. In a large skillet, clarify butter. Pour off all but 2 tablespoons and reserve. In the 2 tablespoons of butter, sauté the chicken pieces, skin-side down, turning carefully until they are brown on all sides. Place them on a heated platter to one side. In the same pan, sauté artichoke hearts, adding more of the clarified butter as necessary, until they are brown; remove to same heated platter. In the same pan add sliced mushrooms, shallots, and garlic, and sauté until the mushrooms are tender and the shallots are translucent. Return the chicken and artichoke hearts to pan, add wine and simmer for 5 minutes, or until chicken pieces are tender. Remove the chicken and vegetables to the heated platter, and thicken the juices in the pan with the arrowroot or flour. Pour sauce over the chicken. Serve with brown rice or bulgur white pilaf. Serves 4.

FRENCH-FRIED TURKEY

LODGE ON THE DESERT, Tucson, Arizona

As patron grande Schuyler Lininger says, "First, you catch a turkey!" This inn is on the edge of the spectacular desert country in southern Arizona and the entire area was once dominated by the hostile Apache Indians. Today it is a haven of rest and quiet with a marvelous view of the Arizona mountains.

BATTER:

1 1/2 cups sifted all-
    purpose flour
2 1/4 tsp. baking powder
3/4 tsp. salt
2 eggs
3/4 cup milk
1 1/2 tbsp. salad oil

Sift flour with baking powder and salt. In medium bowl, with rotary beater, beat eggs, milk, and salad oil until smooth. Gradually add flour mixture, beating until smooth. Yield: 1 1/2 cups.

SAUCE:

1/4 cup butter or
    margarine
1/4 cup unsifted all-
    purpose flour
1 tsp. salt
1/8 tsp. pepper
2 cups milk
2 egg yolks, beaten
1/4 tsp. almond extract

In medium saucepan, slowly heat butter just until melted and golden, not browned, stirring all the while. Remove from heat. Add flour, salt, and pepper; stir until smooth. Add milk, a small amount at a time, stirring after each addition. Return to heat. Over medium heat, bring to boiling, stirring constantly. Reduce heat and add beaten egg yolks, stirring until the mixture thickens. Remove from heat and add almond extract. Yield: 2 1/2 cups.

1/2 turkey breast
    (2 1/2 lbs.), cooked
oil or shortening for frying
slivered toasted almonds

Cut cooked turkey breast into 18 chunks or medallions about 1 1/2" long. Meanwhile, in a deep skillet or deep-fat fryer, slowly heat oil or shortening (at least 2" deep) to 375° on deep-frying thermometer. Dip turkey pieces into batter, coating evenly. Deep-fry a few pieces at a time, turning once, 3 to 4 minutes, or until golden-brown on both sides. Drain well on paper towels. Arrange three pieces per serving on heated platter and ladle sauce over. Sprinkle with slivered toasted almonds. Serves 6.

POULET AU CITRON

1661 INN, Block Island, Rhode Island
What fun it is to visit an inn on an island—Block Island is off the coast of both Connecticut and Rhode Island, and remains virtually the same as it was fifty years ago. Guests at the 1661 Inn enjoy walking on the beaches, biking on the island roads, and especially savoring the delicious dinners served each evening.

Two 2 1/2-lb. chickens, quartered
2 tbsp. grated lemon peel
1/2 cup lemon juice
2 cloves garlic, crushed
2 tsp. crumbled dried thyme
1 1/2 tsp. salt
1 tsp. freshly ground black pepper
1/4 cup butter, melted
1/2 cup chopped parsley for garnish
3 lemons, thinly sliced

Wash chicken and pat dry with paper towels. Transfer chicken to a shallow baking pan large enough to hold the chicken quarters in a single layer. In a small bowl, combine lemon peel, lemon juice, garlic, thyme, salt, and pepper; mix well. Spoon over chicken, turning chicken to coat thoroughly. Refrigerate in marinade 3 to 4 hours, turning chicken pieces several times.

Preheat oven to 425°. Reserving the marinade, remove chicken to paper towels and drain. In a 2-quart baking pan, arrange chicken in a single layer. Brush with melted butter and bake 25 minutes. Brush with reserved marinade. Continue to bake an additional 25 to 30 minutes brushing occasionally with marinade, or until chicken is browned and thoroughly cooked. Transfer to a heated serving platter and garnish with parsley and lemon slices. Heat any remaining marinade to serve as a sauce. Serve with rice. Serves 8.

CHICKEN AND OYSTERS CHAMPAGNE

DOCKSIDE GUEST QUARTERS, York, Maine
York Harbor is a beautiful sight at dawn with its cluster of bobbing lobster boats still tied up at their buoys. All of the rooms in this waterside inn overlook the ever-changing drama of the harbor.

CHICKEN:

1 egg, beaten
1/4 tsp. celery salt
8 6-oz. skinned and boned chicken breasts
flour
6 tbsp. butter

In a shallow pan, combine egg and celery salt. Dredge each chicken breast in flour, shaking off excess. In a 12" skillet, melt the butter and sauté the chicken 6 to 7 minutes on each side. Meanwhile prepare the Oyster and Champagne Sauce.

OYSTER AND CHAMPAGNE SAUCE:

1/2 cup plus 2 tbsp. butter
1/3 cup flour
1 1/2 cups chicken stock
1 1/2 bottles dry
  champagne
1 pt. shucked oysters
2 egg yolks
1/2 cup light cream
salt
freshly ground black
  pepper

In a large saucepan, melt the 1/2 cup butter and stir in flour. Gradually add chicken stock and whisk until thick. Add champagne and simmer very gently 30 minutes or until sauce is thick and reduced by half. Add oysters and cook 5 minutes longer. In a small bowl, beat together egg yolks, remaining 2 tablespoons butter, and cream; then stir egg yolk mixture into the sauce and heat through. Season to taste with salt and pepper. To serve, arrange chicken on a hot platter and pour sauce over chicken. Serves 8.

HASENPFEFFER

LYME INN, Lyme, New Hampshire
Here's a beautiful country inn near the upper Connecticut River where every lodging room is furnished with handsome antiques. This rabbit dish is one of the favorites on the menu.

BRINE:

2 rabbits (6 lbs. total)
  cut up
2 cups dry red wine
1 cup water
1 tbsp. lemon juice
1/2 cup vinegar
1/2 tsp. crumbled dried
  thyme
1/2 tsp. crumbled dried
  marjoram
1/2 tsp. crumbled dried
  rosemary
12 peppercorns
2 stalks celery, minced
4 cloves garlic

In a large glass or enamel bowl, marinate rabbit pieces in brine mixture for two days, turning occasionally. Remove rabbit. Strain and reserve the brine.

1/2 cup flour
salt
4 tsp. butter
4 slices bacon, cut up
1 large onion, diced
1 cup sliced mushrooms
1/2 cup sour cream

Dredge rabbit pieces in mixed flour and salt, shaking off any excess. In a Dutch oven, melt the butter and sauté bacon, onion, and mushrooms. Add the rabbit and sauté until well browned. Pour in reserved brine and simmer until rabbit is tender. Remove from heat and stir in sour cream. Hasenpfeffer may also be cooked in a preheated 375° oven. Serves 6 to 8.

SCALLOPED CHICKEN

DURBIN HOTEL, Rushville, Indiana
Real family-style country cooking is featured at this typical Midwest hostelry.
It was Wendell Willkie's campaign headquarters when he ran for president. This
chicken dish has been a favorite for many years.

3 qts. water
1 tbsp. salt plus salt for
  seasoning
9 oz. uncooked noodles
1/2 cup chicken fat
1/2 cup flour
2 qts. skimmed chicken
  stock
pepper
1 1/2 lbs. cooked chicken,
  diced
1/4 lb. mushrooms, sliced
  and sautéed
1 large pimiento, finely
  chopped
1/4 lb. cheese, grated
1 cup buttered bread
  crumbs
paprika

Preheat oven to 325°. Bring the water and salt to a boil, then cook the noodles 10 minutes. Drain. Mix chicken fat, flour, and a little water to make a smooth paste. In a 3- to 4-quart saucepan, bring the chicken stock to a boil, add the flour mixture and, whisking constantly, simmer 10 minutes or until the sauce is smooth. Salt and pepper to taste. In a large bowl combine the chicken, mushrooms, and pimiento. Add the cooked noodles and mix thoroughly. Transfer to a 6- to 8-quart ovenproof casserole and top with cheese. Pour chicken sauce over the contents of the casserole, top with buttered bread crumbs and sprinkle with paprika. Bake 20 minutes or until top of the scalloped chicken is bubbly and the crumbs are golden. Serves 12.

SOUTHERN FRIED CHICKEN

DOE RUN INN, Brandenburg, Kentucky
Abraham Lincoln's father was one of the workmen on this inn in the early part
of the 19th century. It's a pity that he didn't have the opportunity to enjoy this
delicious chicken treat.

One 2 1/2 lb. fryer chicken
2 tsp. salt
1 1/2 cups lard or
  vegetable oil
2 cups coarse-ground self-
  rising flour

Cut the chicken into eight pieces (2 legs, 2 thighs, 2 wings and 2 half-breasts). In a large bowl, cover the chicken with cold water, add the salt and soak 30 minutes. Meanwhile, in a cast iron skillet, heat the lard or vegetable oil (it should be 1 1/2" deep) until it reaches 370° on a deep-fat frying thermometer. Roll the wet pieces of chicken in the flour. If you like the chicken very crusty, dip in water again and roll in the flour a second time. When the hot fat has reached 370° or when it bubbles when the chicken is placed in the skillet, fry the chicken 15 minutes or until it has a golden crust, then turn the pieces and fry another 10 minutes. Serves 4.

HARE AND MUSHROOM CASSEROLE

CUTTLE'S TREMBLANT INN, Mont Tremblant, Quebec, Canada
If summer is enchanting at this inn with a perfect view of Mont Tremblant across the lake, then winter is magic-time. In addition to Laurentian downhill skiing, there is snowshoeing and excellent cross-country skiing right from the front door of the inn. In summer guests are quite likely to see innkeepers Jim and Betty Cuttle sailing on the lake themselves. Chef Guy Gauthier makes this great casserole when he has some "left-over" roasted hare.

1 cup diced salt pork
1/4 cup bread crumbs
1 medium-sized onion, chopped
1/4 lb. mushrooms, sliced
1/4 cup chopped parsley
1 roasted hare, cut up
salt
freshly ground black pepper
butter
1 cup consommé

Preheat oven to 325°. In a medium-sized skillet, brown diced salt pork and transfer to a 3-quart ovenproof casserole. Cover with half the bread crumbs, onions, mushrooms, and parsley. Over this layer place the pieces of hare and cover with remaining onions, mushrooms, parsley, and salt and pepper to taste. Sprinkle with remaining bread crumbs and dot with butter. Pour consommé over contents of casserole. Bake 20 to 30 minutes or until the sauce is thick and bubbly. Serves 4.

QUAIL WITH MADEIRA SAUCE

CHARLOTTE INN, Edgartown, Massachusetts
The former home of a Martha's Vineyard sea captain, today it's a combination inn, art gallery, and French restaurant. Gery Conover has made this a most delightful place to stay—beautifully decorated with every comfort.

Four 4-oz. domestic quail
1 clove garlic
salt
freshly ground black pepper
2 tbsp. butter
1/4 cup Madeira wine
1/2 cup chicken stock
1 tbsp. flour

Preheat oven to 400°. Wash and trim each quail, discarding the necks. Split quail along the backbone. Rub skin with garlic and season with salt and pepper. In a heavy 10 to 12" skillet, melt the butter and brown quail 5 to 7 minutes. Transfer quail, breast side up, to an ovenproof, lidded casserole. Deglaze the skillet with Madeira, scraping bottom and sides of skillet. Add chicken stock and simmer 3 minutes. Pour this liquid over quail, cover, and cook in oven 15 minutes. Remove lid and cook 5 minutes longer. Transfer quail to a warmed platter. Thicken juices remaining in casserole with flour and pour wine sauce over quail. Serve immediately. Serves 2.

PEANUT DRESSING

WAYSIDE INN, Middletown, Virginia

Located at the northern end of the luxuriant Shenandoah Valley on the gorgeous Skyline Drive, this inn has known the excitement of both the American Revolution and the War Between the States. A few years ago, the innkeeper discovered a heretofore-unknown slave kitchen which is now used as one of the many dining rooms.

1/2 cup butter
1/2 cup celery, chopped
1/2 cup onion, chopped
1/4 bunch parsley,
  chopped
1 cup water
  (may need more)
1/2 lb. chicken giblets,
  chopped
2 tsp. salt
1/8 tsp. pepper
4 cups bread crumbs
1 tsp. sage
1 tsp. poultry seasoning
1 cup chopped peanuts

Preheat oven to 350°. In a skillet melt the butter. Sauté the celery, onion, and parsley until tender. In a large saucepan bring the water to a boil. Add the chopped giblets, salt, pepper, and sautéed vegetable mixture. Simmer 1 hour. Meanwhile, in a large bowl combine the bread crumbs, sage and poultry seasoning. Strain giblet stock and blend giblets and vegetables in a blender. Combine this mixture with the stock and pour over the bread crumb mixture. Add peanuts. Transfer dressing into a 9x5x3" loaf pan and bake 1 hour or use as stuffing for turkey.

RICE-ALMOND STUFFING

THE COUNTRY CLUB INN, Rangeley, Maine

Bob and Sue Crory describe the Country Club Inn as being surrounded by mountains of golf. It is located on a 2,000-foot promontory with a view worth $24,000,000 a year, according to the state assessor. The golf is just 25 steps away to the first tee, and the inn enjoys breathtaking views of Rangeley Lake and the beautiful mountains. Can you imagine what it's like during the fall foliage season?

1/4 cup melted butter
2 cups cooked wild rice
1/4 cup sliced almonds
1/4 tsp. minced garlic
salt
pepper
1/4 cup finely chopped
  apples

In a 10" skillet, sauté all ingredients, except the apples, in the butter until the almonds are brown. Remove from heat and add the apples. Use to stuff chicken breasts. Also very good with sole fillets or haddock. Yield: 2 1/2 cups stuffing.

MEATS

BRADFORD GARDENS INN

HERITAGE HOUSE

THE WHITE HART INN

CUTE DE VEAU NORMANDE

SWISS HUTTE, Hillsdale, New York
The English translation for this dish is "veal chops with mushrooms and cream," and it makes a delicious entrée. The Swiss Hutte is a Bavarian inn that overlooks the Catamount ski area in eastern New York State.

4 veal chops, 3/4-inch thick (about 2 lbs.)
1 tbsp. vegetable oil
salt
pepper
4 tbsp. butter
2 tbsp. minced shallots or green onion
1/2 cup dry white wine
1/2 cup chicken broth
1 cup sliced fresh mushrooms
1 cup whipping cream
2 tsp. arrowroot
1/4 cup apple brandy
1/4 tsp. salt
1/8 tsp. pepper

Preheat oven to 400°. In an ovenproof skillet, brown chops in hot oil 5 minutes per side. Season with salt and pepper. Remove and set aside. Pour off fat. To skillet add 2 tablespoons of the butter and shallots; cook till tender but not brown. Add white wine and reduce to a glaze (about 2 tablespoons). Add chicken broth. Return chops to skillet; spoon juices over. Cover and bake for 15 minutes. Meanwhile in small saucepan, cook mushrooms in remaining 2 tablespoons butter for 2 minutes. Remove mushrooms and set aside. In a small bowl, mix cream and arrowroot. To heated skillet, add brandy; flame. After flame subsides add cream mixture; cook and stir till mixture thickens. Season to taste with salt and pepper, and add mushrooms. Spoon sauce over chops and serve. Serves 4.

TOURTIÈRE
(French Canadian Pork Pie)

BRADFORD GARDENS INN, Provincetown, Massachusetts
This village at the end of Cape Cod is both bizarre and intriguing. Each of the Bradford Gardens lodging rooms has its own character, and many have fireplaces. The grounds are distinguished by having over 300 rose bushes and flowering fruit trees.

1 lb. ground lean pork
1/2 lb. ground lean beef
3 tbsp. minced onion
1/2 tsp. salt
1/8 tsp. freshly ground black pepper
1 cup water
1/8 tsp. ground cloves
1/4 tsp. ground cinnamon
1 1/2 cup mashed potatoes (2 medium)
pastry for one 9" two-crust pie, see recipe in Pies

In a 10 to 12" cast iron skillet, combine pork, beef, onion, salt, pepper, and water. Simmer over low heat 45 minutes. Add cloves and cinnamon and cook 15 minutes longer. Add potatoes, combine and cool thoroughly—about 1 hour.

Preheat oven to 400°. Line a 9" pie pan with pastry. Fill the pie with the ground meat mixture, cover with remaining dough, cut vents and flute edges. Bake 45 minutes. Tourtière freezes well and is best served with raw cranberry-orange relish. Yield: One 9" pork pie.

GINGER-GLAZED CORNED BEEF

HERITAGE HOUSE, Little River, California
"It's like a lovely dream," said one guest of this beautiful inn with its unobstructed view of the Pacific Ocean. And about the ginger-glazed corned beef: "It's incredible!"

1 corned beef, preferably
  eye of the round
1 lb. brown sugar
3 cups water
1/2 cup slivered
  crystalized ginger

Prepare the corned beef according to directions on package. Preheat oven to 350°. In a 3-quart saucepan, combine brown sugar and water and cook until mixture becomes syrupy. Stir in crystalized ginger and cook several minutes longer. Reserving some glaze to pour over each portion of corned beef, pour remaining glaze over beef and bake 15 minutes.

BEEF STEW WITH HOMEMADE BAKING POWDER BISCUITS

STERLING INN, South Sterling, Pennsylvania
There's a waterfall, a rippling creek, a putting green, tennis courts, and woodland walks at this secluded inn on a back road in the Poconos. Carmen Arneberg says their meals are the kind that "some people serve only when they are having guests for dinner."

BEEF STEW:

3 tbsp. shortening
2 lb. lean beef, cubed and
  dredged in flour
4 medium-sized onions,
  quartered, or 8 whole
  small onions
3 carrots, scraped and cut
  in 1" pieces
1 cup 1" celery slices
3 medium-sized potatoes,
  peeled and quartered
1 1-lb. can tomatoes,
  drained and chopped
1 10-oz. package frozen
  green peas
1 tbsp. Worcestershire
  sauce
2 tsp. salt
1/4 cup flour plus 1/2 cup
  water combined into a
  paste

In a Dutch oven, melt shortening and brown beef cubes on all sides. Add 2 cups water, cover and simmer 2 hours, stirring occasionally. Add 2 more cups water, onions, carrots, and celery and cook until vegetables are just tender. Add potatoes, tomatoes, peas, Worcestershire, and salt. Cook 20 minutes, adding more water if necessary. Thicken the stew with flour and water paste. Heat through, stirring. Serve over wide noodles or hot Homemade Baking Powder biscuits. Serves 6.

HOMEMADE BAKING POWDER BISCUITS:

2 cups flour
5 tbsp. shortening
1 tbsp. baking powder
1/2 tsp. salt
3/4 cup milk

Preheat oven to 400°. In a large mixing bowl, with a pastry blender combine flour, shortening, baking powder, and salt. Add milk and stir the dough until it is thoroughly blended. Turn out onto a floured board and knead 1 minute. Roll out 1/2" thick and cut with a 2" cookie cutter. Bake 15 minutes. Yield: 10 biscuits.

MANDARIN SWEET AND SOUR PORK

THE WHITE HART INN, Salisbury, Connecticut
Splendidly situated in the northwest corner of Connecticut in the foothills of the Berkshires, the White Hart is the "local" for the people living in Lakeville, Sharon, Canaan, and Salisbury. The genial innkeeper, John Harney, is known not only for his wit, but for offering New England and Oriental fare. Here is one of Chef Yu Shan Lee's specialties.

SWEET AND SOUR SAUCE:

4 tbsp. vegetable oil
1 3/4 cups tomato ketchup
4 oz. sweet white
   cucumber, sliced*
1/2 cup red wine vinegar
1 cup chicken stock
2/3 cup sugar
1/2 cup honey
1 20-oz. can lichee nuts*
3 tbsp. cornstarch
   combined with 1/2 cup
   water

In a 3-quart saucepan, heat vegetable oil and add ketchup, cucumber, vinegar, chicken stock, honey, and lichee nuts. Bring to a boil and add the cornstarch and water mixture; cook until sauce thickens slightly. If the color is too pale, add red food coloring. Keep warm while you prepare the pork.

DEEP FRIED PORK:

1/2 cup flour
1 egg
1 tbsp. baking powder
1 tbsp. soy sauce
1 cup water
2 lbs. lean pork or fresh
   ham, cut in 1 1/2" strips
6 cups oil for deep fat
   frying

In a medium-sized bowl, thoroughly combine flour, egg, baking powder, soy sauce, and water. Dip the pork strips in batter, coating them well. Heat the oil for deep frying until it reaches 375° on a deep fat thermometer. Carefully slide the pork strips into the fat, cooking them until they are dark brown and crispy on the outside, but still tender. Pour the prepared sauce over the pork and serve at once. Serves 6.

Diced pineapple, green pepper, etc., may be substituted for the white cucumber and lichee nuts.

GOULASH

MILLHOF INN, Stephentown, New York
Here's an American country inn with a real central European flavor because Ronnie Tallet is from Yugoslavia and her husband Frank is from France. The inn looks like many Black Forest hostelries that I have visited. This goulash is one of many tasty main dishes which Ronnie creates in her own kitchen.

1/2 cup oil
12 medium-sized onions, coarsely chopped
3 lbs. lean chuck, cut in 1" cubes
1 bay leaf
1 tsp. caraway seeds
1/2 cup dry red wine
3/4 cup water
1/4 tsp. crumbled dried basil
1 tsp. salt
1/4 tsp. freshly ground pepper
1 tsp. tomato paste
1 tsp. Hungarian paprika

In a Dutch oven, heat the oil, then sauté the onions until they are golden. Add beef, bay leaf, and caraway seeds, stirring to combine the ingredients. Simmer over low heat; do not cover. When the pan juices have been absorbed, add the wine first and then some water, as needed. After 2 1/2 hours, stir in basil, salt and pepper, tomato paste, and remaining water. Cover and simmer 20 minutes longer, or until the beef is tender. Remove and discard bay leaf. Stir in the paprika. Serve with thin noodles. Serves 6.

BEEF BALLS BORDELAISE

CLARKSON HOUSE, Lewiston, New York
This western New York restaurant is just minutes from the grandeur of Niagara Falls. The menu has been judiciously pared down to a few entrées which are very carefully and most tastefully prepared. The walls of this inn are decorated with tools and gadgets used over a hundred years ago—Marilyn Clarkson says uses have not been discovered for some of them.

MEATBALLS:

1 lb. lean ground beef
1 1/2 cups seasoned bread crumbs
1 tbsp. finely chopped green pepper
1 tbsp. finely chopped onion
1/2 tsp. salt
1/2 tsp. dry mustard
pinch crumbled dried thyme
freshly ground pepper (5 or 6 twists)

In a medium-sized bowl, combine all the meatball ingredients and shape into 1"-diameter balls. In a 10 to 12" skillet, sauté the meatballs transferring them to a plate as they are browned.

BORDELAISE SAUCE:

Reserved pan juices from
   sautéed meatballs
2 shallots, thinly sliced
1 tbsp. flour
1 1/2 cups beef bouillon
1 tbsp. tomato ketchup
1 tbsp. Worcestershire
   sauce
1/4 cup red wine

In the reserved pan juices sauté the shallots until they are translucent. Add remaining sauce ingredients to the skillet, whisking constantly. When sauce is heated through, transfer the meatballs to the skillet and simmer 1/2 hour. Yield: Two dozen 1" meatballs.

HAM LOAF WITH HORSERADISH SAUCE

CENTURY INN, Scenery Hill, Pennsylvania
Known for its air of warm hospitality and huge, homecooked meals, this inn is filled with rare antiques and pervaded with a sense of history. This recipe is on the Century Inn's party menu, and with the glazed surface and the ribbon of horseradish, it makes a handsome entrée, as well as a delicious one.

HAM LOAF:

3 lbs. ground ham
1 1/2 lb. ground fresh pork
3 eggs
4 cups soft bread crumbs
mayonnaise
2 cups firmly packed
   brown sugar
1 cup vinegar
1 tbsp. dry mustard
2 1/2 cups water
4 or 5 baking potatoes
   (optional)

Preheat oven to 350°. In a large mixing bowl, combine ground meats, eggs, bread crumbs and sufficient mayonnaise to moisten the mixture. Using 1 to 1 1/2 cups per loaf, shape into individual loaves; or shape into one large loaf. Place the small loaves in a shallow roasting pan, side by side, but not touching; the large loaf may be baked in a shallow roasting pan, also. In a 2-quart saucepan, combine and bring to a boil the remaining ingredients. Pour some of the mixture over the ham loaves, reserving sufficient liquid with which to baste the loaves frequently as they cook. Bake 45 minutes to 1 hour for individual loaves, slightly longer for a large loaf. Baking potatoes, pared and cut in half lengthwise, may be placed around the meat and turned in the juices as the meat is basted. The remaining basting sauce may be served with the potatoes. Serves 10.

HORSERADISH SAUCE:

1 pt. sour cream
horseradish
onion salt

Combine the sour cream with horseradish and onion salt to taste. When you are ready to serve the ham loaves place one teaspoon sauce In a ribbon over each individual loaf or spread all of the sauce on the large loaf.

YANKEE POT ROAST

LONGFELLOW'S WAYSIDE INN, South Sudbury, Massachusetts
The militia men of South Sudbury gathered on the site of this inn in 1775 to acquire both courage and refreshment before marching on to oppose the British at nearby Concord. Today it is a well-preserved and restored inn, made famous by the American poet, Henry Wadsworth Longfellow, in his famous Tales of A Wayside Inn.

1 4 to 6-lb. bottom of the round roast
salt
pepper
1/2 cup vegetable oil
3 celery stalks, coarsely chopped
2 carrots, sliced
1 small onion
3 or 4 fresh tomatoes or 1 1-lb. can tomatoes

Preheat the oven to 450°. In a Dutch oven in vegetable oil braise the beef in the oven 30 minutes, turning occasionally. Salt and pepper to taste. Add the vegetables and cook 10 minutes longer. Then, cover the meat with water, cover the pot, remove from oven and simmer on top of stove 2 1/2 to 3 hours, or until the meat is tender. Remove beef from the Dutch oven and set aside. Strain and reserve the remaining liquid stock for the Jardinière Sauce. Cool. Skim off fat.

JARDINIÈRE SAUCE:

1/2 cup butter
1/2 cup flour
3 cups liquid stock
salt
pepper
1/3 cup cooked peas
1/3 cup cooked, cubed carrots
1 celery stalk, sliced and braised in butter 2-3 minutes

In a large saucepan, melt the butter, whisk in the flour and gradually pour in stock, whisking constantly. Season to taste with salt and pepper. Just before serving add the vegetables to the sauce and heat through. To serve, slice beef 1/3" thick, place on a heated platter and cover with Jardinière Sauce. Serves 8.

PAUPIETTES DE VEAU AUX DUXELLES, SAUCE BÉARNAISE

INN AT PRINCETON, Princeton, Massachusetts
From the porch of this inn, it's possible to see the twinkling lights of Boston, some forty miles distant. The rooms are spacious and furnished with style. Dinners are usually by candlelight, and this dish (which translates to Veal Rolls with Mushroom Stuffing) is served with rice pilaf and fresh vegetables.

1 1/2 lbs. veal, cut from the leg in 8 slices
salt
pepper
4 eggs
1 tbsp. milk
flour for dredging
8 tbsp. clarified butter*

Prepare Duxelles and Sauce Béarnaise. Preheat oven to 350°. Place veal slices between waxed paper and with a flat mallet pound thin. Season with salt and pepper. In a shallow bowl, combine eggs and milk. Dredge veal slices in flour, then dip in egg batter. In large skillet, heat butter. (If more than one skillet is necessary,

1 1/2 cups Duxelles (below)
juice of 1 lemon
dry white wine to taste
1 1/2 cups Sauce Béarnaise
(below)

divide butter evenly—more may be required.) Quickly sauté egg-coated veal slices in hot, but not browned, butter, until golden on both sides. Transfer to cutting board or working surface. Place spoonful of Duxelles at one end of veal slice and roll up, securing with a toothpick. Return veal to skillet and add lemon juice and wine to taste. Bake in oven 10 to 15 minutes, or until heated through. Remove toothpicks. Transfer Veal Paupiettes to warmed serving platter and top with Sauce Béarnaise. Serves 4.

DUXELLES:

1 medium onion, diced
  fine
1 tbsp. minced garlic
1/2 lb. mushrooms, diced
  fine
1 tbsp. chopped parsley
1 tbsp. chopped chives
1 tsp. ground nutmeg
1 tsp. crumbled dried
  thyme
1 tbsp. port wine
1 tbsp. brandy
1 tbsp. dry white wine
5 tbsp. clarified butter*
2 tbsp. unflavored bread
  crumbs

In a 10 to 12" skillet, sauté onions and garlic in butter until tender, add the rest of ingredients and cook until most of the moisture is absorbed. Remove from heat and add bread crumbs, combining thoroughly. Refrigerate in a covered container. Yield: 1 1/2 cups Duxelles.

SAUCE BÉARNAISE:

3 tbsp. tarragon vinegar
1 tbsp. chopped tarragon
  leaves
3 tbsp. dry white wine
1 tsp. chopped parsley
1 tsp. chopped chervil
1 tsp. minced shallots
1 tsp. Worcestershire
  sauce
3 egg yolks
3/4 cup melted butter
salt
pepper

In a small saucepan, combine all ingredients, except eggs, butter, and salt and pepper. Cooking over moderate heat, reduce to 1/3 cup liquid. Let cool briefly. Transfer to double boiler over hot, but not boiling, water. Add egg yolks and whisk until mixture is hot and creamy. Add melted butter slowly, mixing thoroughly. Remove sauce from heat, season with salt and pepper to taste, and keep warm until ready to serve. Yield: 1 1/2 cups Sauce Béarnaise.

*To clarify butter, start with more butter than the recipe calls for. Melt butter in saucepan over low heat. Remove from heat and cool. Remove yellow, foamy surface fat. What remains is clarified butter; however, do not use milk solids at bottom of the pan.

STUFFED PORK CHOPS

WILDERNESS LODGE, Lesterville, Missouri

For people who love horseback riding, floating, platform tennis, canoeing, hiking, fishing, and other outdoor activities, the Wilderness Lodge in the Missouri Ozarks, is ideal. Such vigorous outdoor activity naturally encourages gargantuan appetites and this recipe for Stuffed Pork Chops is designed to relieve the hunger pains!

STUFFING PER CHOP:

2 tbsp. butter, plus 2 tbsp. for frying
1 tsp. coarsely chopped green pepper
1 tsp. coarsely chopped celery
1 tsp. coarsely chopped onion
1/2 cup crumbled cornbread
salt
freshly ground black pepper
pinch garlic powder
1/2 tsp. poultry seasoning
milk
1 1-lb. double cut pork chop with pocket per person

Preheat oven to 350°. In a small skillet, melt 2 tablespoons of the butter and sauté vegetables. In a small bowl, combine cornbread and sautéed vegetables, then add salt and pepper to taste, garlic powder and poultry seasoning. Cool. Add sufficient milk for ingredients to be moist but not soggy. Pack stuffing firmly into pork chop pocket. In the remaining 2 tablespoons butter fry chop until golden brown. Place on a rack in roasting pan and add enough hot water to cause steam. Steam in oven 1 hour to 1 hour 15 minutes, or until chop falls from fork when pierced. Serves 1.

PORK PICCATA

EDSON HILL MANOR, Stowe, Vermont

A gracious, homelike atmosphere with a sense of casual luxury prevails here in fireplaced rooms with pine-panelled walls and floor-to-ceiling windows with attractive draperies. This mountain hideaway is in the center of an extremely popular skiing and resort area in northern Vermont.

2 1/2 lbs. center pork loin boned and trimmed
salt
white pepper
flour
4 eggs, beaten
1/2 cup grated Parmesan cheese
1/4 cup parsley, chopped
butter and oil for sautéeing

Preheat oven to 350°. Remove all fat and membrane from pork, slice 1/4-inch thick and flatten slightly with a meat tenderizer or cleaver. Season cutlets and dredge in flour, shaking off all excess. In a medium-sized bowl, combine eggs, cheese, and parsley. Mix well and allow to stand several minutes. Dip cutlets into batter, which should coat and cling to pork easily. If batter is too thin, add more cheese, if too thick, add a little cream. Sauté cutlets until golden brown on both sides in 3 parts of very hot butter and 1 part very hot oil. Transfer to a baking pan and cook in the oven 5 minutes. Serves 6.

WILDERNESS LODGE

INN AT PRINCETON

EDSON HILL MANOR

HANDFIELD INN

VILLAGE INN

GOLDEN LAMB

RUMP OF VEAL ST. MARC

HANDFIELD INN, St. Marc-sur-le-Richelieu, Quebec, Canada
Here's a real French inn just an hour from Montreal in a village that you would expect to find anywhere in France. This is one of the favorites from an extensive menu, prepared by Chef Antonin Gatien. He advises serving it with a tall glass of cold beer!

4 lbs. boned rump of veal
salt
pepper
6 tbsp. butter
1 onion, diced
1 carrot, diced
1 celery stalk, diced
3 10-oz. bottles of beer
1 clove garlic, crushed
pinch of crumbled, dried thyme
1 bay leaf
1 tbsp. tomato paste
2 tbsp. flour
1 cup light whipping cream

Preheat oven to 325°. Season meat with salt and pepper. In a heavy braiser brown veal on all sides in 4 tablespoons of the butter. Add vegetables and sauté a few minutes. Pour 2 bottles of beer over the meat. Add garlic, thyme, bay leaf, salt and pepper to taste, and tomato paste. Cover and cook in oven until veal is tender, about 2 hours, adding the remaining bottle of beer gradually as the cooking juice reduces. When veal is tender remove the meat to a platter and keep hot. Reduce cooking juice, thickening it with the remaining 2 tablespoons of butter kneaded with flour. Add cream. Taste for seasoning and cover meat with sauce. Serves 8.

BORDELAISE SAUCE

VILLAGE INN, Landgrove, Vermont
Children can have a ball here—the atmosphere is perfect for families, with a variety of room arrangements, and there are no end of activities and recreational pursuits in these central Vermont mountains. Kathy Snyder says this sauce is super over roast beef, and suggests you make it the day before you need it.

2 tbsp. butter
1 slice onion
2 slices carrot
sprig parsley
6 whole black peppercorns
1 whole clove
1/2 bay leaf
2 tbsp. flour
1 10 1/2-oz. can condensed beef bouillon
1/4 tsp. salt
1/8 tsp. pepper
1/4 cup dry red wine
1 tbsp. snipped parsley

In a 10" skillet, in hot butter, sauté onion, carrot, parsley, peppercorns, clove, and bay leaf until onion is tender. Add flour and cook over low heat, stirring, until browned. Stir in bouillon and simmer, stirring occasionally, for 10 minutes, or until thickened. Strain into lidded container, add salt, pepper, red wine, and parsley. Cover tightly and refrigerate until needed. Yield: 1 1/2 cups Bordelaise Sauce.

BRAISED LAMB SHANKS

GOLDEN LAMB, Lebanon, Ohio

This lovely old inn in the heartland of America has been playing host to distinguished visitors for 170 years—the list includes Charles Dickens and several American presidents, among others. This recipe for lamb shanks is one of their most popular dishes.

4 15- to 16-oz. lamb shanks
3 tbsp. shortening
1 large onion, diced
1 cup mushrooms, halved
   or quartered
3/4 cup celery cut into
   1x1/4" slices
1 turnip, peeled and cut
   into 1x1/4" slices
3 tbsp. tomato paste
5 tbsp. flour
1/4 tsp. black pepper
pinch dried rosemary
   leaves, finely crumbled
pinch dried thyme leaves,
   crumbled
1 bay leaf
2 cloves garlic, minced
1/2 cup Burgundy wine
6 cups lamb stock
   (or substitute beef stock)
chopped parsley for
   garnish

Preheat oven to 325°. Season lamb shanks with salt and pepper. In a heavy braiser, melt the shortening and brown the lamb on all sides. Add the vegetables and brown. Mix the tomato paste into the braiser and stir in the flour, browning lightly. Season with rosemary, thyme, bay leaf, garlic, and black pepper. Pour in Burgundy and lamb or beef stock. Cover the braiser, place in oven and, skimming off the fat occasionally, cook the lamb 1 to 1 1/2 hours. Discard bay leaf. Correct seasoning. To serve, transfer the lamb shanks to a heated platter, cover with sauce, and garnish with parsley. Serves 4.

VEGETABLES

GENERAL LEWIS INN

WATERFORD INNE

HEMLOCK INN

BROCCOLI CASSEROLE

GENERAL LEWIS INN, Lewisburg, West Virginia

With this recipe served at this historic inn in the West Virginia mountains, the humble broccoli stalk attains new heights of acclaim. I have had many compliments on it when I serve it in Massachusetts.

2 10-oz. pkgs. frozen
   chopped broccoli
1 tbsp. butter
1 tbsp. minced onion
1 10 1/2-oz. can cream of
   mushroom soup
1/3 cup milk
1/3 cup grated cheese
1 egg
1/2 cup buttered bread
   crumbs

Cook broccoli according to directions on package. Drain. Preheat oven to 350°. In a 3-quart saucepan, melt butter and cook onion until it is translucent. Pour in mushroom soup and milk. Add cheese. Heat until cheese is melted, then whisk in the egg. Combine the broccoli and sauce and transfer to a 9x13" baking dish. Sprinkle with the buttered bread crumbs and bake 30 minutes or until the sauce bubbles and the crumbs are brown. Serves 6.

ZUCCHINI SQUARES

WATERFORD INNE, East Waterford, Maine

The Waterford Inn, which commands a most attractive view of western Maine's Oxford Hills, is owned and operated by a mother-daughter team who originally lived in Oradell, New Jersey. They have created a warm and generous country inn that even in a short period of time has a reputation for good food and geniune hospitality.

1 cup Bisquick
1/2 cup chopped onion
1/2 cup grated Parmesan
   cheese
3 tbsp. chopped parsley
1/2 tsp. salt
1/2 tsp. crumbled dried
   marjoram
pinch freshly ground black
   pepper
1 clove garlic, finely
   chopped
1/2 cup vegetable oil
4 eggs, slightly beaten
3 cups thinly sliced
   zucchini

Preheat oven to 350°. Grease a 13x9x2" pan. In a large mixing bowl, combine all ingredients, adding zucchini last. Transfer to prepared pan. Bake 30 minutes or until golden brown. When cool, cut into 2x1" squares. Yield: 12 squares.

May also be cut into smaller squares and served as an appetizer.

SAUERKRAUT AND BAKED BEANS

THE TAVERN, New Wilmington, Pennsylvania
Located in the heart of western Pennsylvania's "Dutch Country," the Tavern, which has been run by Mrs. Ernst Durrast for over forty years, is a particular favorite for people who enjoy hearty country food in most generous quantities. New Wilmington is just a few minutes from I-80, the east-west highway that traverses northern Pennsylvania.

1 2-lb. can sauerkraut
2 slices bacon
1 small onion, chopped
1 apple (peeled or
 unpeeled), chopped
1 1-lb. can baked beans
1 cup sour cream
2 tsp. caraway seeds

Wash, drain, and chop sauerkraut. In a Dutch oven, cook bacon and onion. Stir in sauerkraut. Cover with water. Add apple. Cook slowly 2 or 3 hours. Add baked beans. About 15 minutes before serving, stir in sour cream and caraway seeds. Serves 12.

OKRA FRITTERS

HEMLOCK INN, Bryson City, North Carolina
Family-style meals served at large Lazy Susan tables characterize the atmosphere in this family-run inn, high in the foothills of the Great Smokies. Sitting and admiring the magnificent view is a favorite pastime for those who eschew more strenuous activities.

1 cup self-rising cornmeal
1 10-oz. package frozen
 okra, chopped
fat for deep frying

Combine cornmeal and sufficient water to form a thick batter. Add okra. Drop by spoonful into hot fat and deep fry until golden brown. Serves 8.

SPINACH SOUFFLE

LINCKLAEN HOUSE, Cazenovia, New York
This inn, located on the edge of the Finger Lakes in one of the attractive towns on Route 20 in central New York State, is a beautifully preserved example of early 19th-century Greek Revival architecture. Its vivacious and innovative innkeeper, Helen Tobin, serves afternoon tea at the inn every day. This recipe could be an elegant vegetable dish for a dinner party.

6 tbsp. butter
6 tbsp. flour
3 tsp. grated onion
3/4 tsp. salt
1/8 tsp. pepper
1 tsp. nutmeg
1 1/2 cups milk
1 3-lb. pkg. frozen spinach
6 large eggs, separated

Preheat oven to 300°. Melt butter in top of double boiler over direct heat. Remove from heat. Blend in flour, onion, salt, pepper, and nutmeg. Slowly stir in milk. Cook over direct heat stirring constantly until mixture thickens and boils for 1 min. Add block of frozen spinach. Cover. Place over boiling water. Heat, stirring with fork

occasionally to break block apart, 20 minutes or until spinach is completely thawed. In medium-sized bowl beat egg whites until stiff enough to form soft peaks. In another bowl, beat egg yolks. Slowly stir into spinach mixture. Gently fold in beaten egg whites. Pour into buttered shallow casserole. Bake 45 minutes or until soufflé is firm in center and knife inserted comes out clean. Serves 20.

TOMATO PIE

INN ON THE LIBRARY LAWN, Westport, New York
Situated on the western shores of Lake Champlain, Westport is a quiet, conservative village—and a regular stop on Amtrak. The inn has high-ceilinged, Victorian bedrooms, some of which look over a lawn to the Lake. Guests enjoy tennis and golf, as well as cross-country skiing.

1 9" unbaked pie crust,
  see recipe in Pies
8 large ripe tomatoes
salt
pepper
1/4 cup (scant) chopped
  chives
2 tbsp. fresh basil,
  chopped
1 cup mayonnaise
1 cup grated cheddar
  cheese

Preheat oven to 400°. Drop tomatoes in boiling water for 10 seconds to loosen skins and peel. After slicing allow to drain, if very juicy. Fill pie crust with tomato slices, mounding towards center. Sprinkle with salt, pepper, chives, and basil. In a small bowl, mix mayonnaise with cheese and spread over the tomatoes. Bake for 35 minutes. To prevent overbrowning, cover with foil for the last 10 minutes. Good with broiled fish or steak. Serves 6.

SQUASH SOUFFLÉ

INN AT PLEASANT HILL, Shakertown, Kentucky
Shakertown is a Shaker community with over twenty lovingly and faithfully restored Shaker buildings. This recipe is from the authentic Shakertown cookbook, We Make You Kindly Welcome.

2 lbs. squash (yellow or
  zucchini)
1 onion, sliced
3 tbsp. butter
3 eggs, beaten
1 can cream of mushroom
  soup
3/4 tsp. salt
1/2 tsp. pepper
cracker crumbs
Parmesan cheese

Preheat oven to 350°. Butter casserole dish. Cook squash and onion until tender. Drain and mash. Fold in remaining ingredients. Place in casserole dish and top with cracker crumbs and Parmesan cheese. Bake for 30 minutes. Serves 6.

STAFFORD'S BAY VIEW INN

THE BURN

LINCKLAEN HOUSE

TOMATO PUDDING

STAFFORD'S BAY VIEW INN, Bay View, Michigan

The Bay View section of Petoskey in northern Michigan is a uniquely preserved Victorian township where the quiet elegance of the turn of the century is still gracefully intact. Innkeepers Janice and Stafford Smith grew up in Bay View. Janice tells me this recipe is from the old Dilworth Inn at Horton Bay. She sometimes adds some drained tomatoes and a little sweet basil, and toasts the bread.

1 10-oz. can tomato purée
1/2 cup boiling water
1 cup firmly packed brown
  sugar
1/4 tsp. salt
1 cup cubed white bread
1/2 cup butter, melted

Preheat oven to 375°. In a 2-quart saucepan, combine tomato purée, boiling water, brown sugar, and salt. Bring to a boil and cook 5 minutes. Place bread cubes in a 2-quart casserole equipped with a lid and pour melted butter over them, piercing the cubes with a fork so that they absorb the butter. Cover the bread with the tomato mixture, piercing again with a fork. Bake, covered, 30 minutes. Serves 6.

GARLIC GRITS

THE BURN, Natchez, Mississippi

Built in 1832, the Burn is a marvelously preserved example of antebellum architecture in one of Mississippi's most historic towns. Each of the four bedrooms is furnished with elegant antiques, including four-poster beds with intricately carved wooden canopies. Guests are served sumptuous plantation-style breakfasts on the terrace overlooking the gardens.

3 cups water
3/4 tsp. salt
1 cup grits
1 6-oz. roll garlic cheese
1/4 cup butter
2 eggs, beaten
1/4 cup milk
cayenne pepper
1/2 cup grated sharp
  cheese
paprika

Preheat oven to 300°. Grease an 8x10" baking dish. Bring water to a boil with salt and cook grits 5 minutes or until done. Add garlic cheese, butter, eggs, milk, and cayenne pepper to taste. Bake 45 minutes, then top with grated cheese and paprika. Return to oven until cheese has melted. Serves 8.

BASIL AND CAPER SAUCE

THE PENTAGOET INN, Castine, Maine

Castine, Maine is one of the most undiscovered places in North America, and the Pentagoet Inn is a cozy, intimate place which sits above the harbor. It has been brought to life by its owner/innkeeper Natalie Saunders who delights in sharing a lifestyle so often forgotten in today's busy world. Built in 1894, this Victorian inn offers the appeal of a bygone era—here time does, indeed, appear to stand still.

5 strips bacon
3/4 lb. butter
1/3 cup capers, chopped
1/4 cup dry white wine
1/3 cup tarragon vinegar
6 fresh basil leaves,
  chopped
1/2 pt. heavy cream
1/2 cup pimientos,
  chopped

Sauté bacon until crisp, drain on paper towels, and chop. Melt butter over high heat. Add bacon, capers, wine, and vinegar. Cook for 10 minutes. Add basil, cream, and pimiento and cook until basil is tender. Serve.over steamed vegetables. Serves 12.

BRUNCH
AND LUNCHEON
DISHES

BEEKMAN ARMS

MAINSTAY INN

NAUSET HOUSE

EGGPLANT DI CARNEVALLE

BEEKMAN ARMS, Rhinebeck, New York
Proclaimed as America's oldest inn, the Beekman Arms has offered its hospitality to many American presidents, educators, and men and women of letters. Today, visitors delight in lunches or dinners in the low-ceilinged taproom where there is a collection of long-stemmed Dutch clay pipes. This dish makes a fine entrée for a luncheon party, or it can be frozen for various future meals.

4 large eggplants, sliced
   crosswise 1/4" thick
1 lb. flour
12 eggs, beaten, plus 3 eggs
8 cups bread crumbs
hot oil for sautéeing
3 lbs. frozen spinach,
   chopped
2 1/4 lbs. ricotta cheese
3 tbsp. grated Parmesan
   cheese
4 tbsp. oregano
2 tbsp. minced garlic
2 tbsp. minced basil
salt
freshly ground black
   pepper
1 1/2 qts. tomato sauce
2 lbs. mozzarella cheese,
   sliced

Preheat oven to 350°. Dredge eggplant in flour, dip into beaten eggs, then coat with bread crumbs. Sauté in hot oil until lightly browned. Drain on absorbent paper. Coat a large, 2 1/2-inch-deep baking pan with oil. In a large mixing bowl, combine remaining 3 eggs, spinach, ricotta and Parmesan cheeses, oregano, garlic, and basil. Season to taste with salt and pepper. Spread 1/2 of the tomato sauce on bottom of prepared baking pan. Place half the eggplant slices over the tomato sauce; cover with half the cheese and spinach mixture and a thin layer of tomato sauce. Top with half the mozzarella cheese slices. Repeat, ending with a layer of mozzarella. Cover with aluminum foil and bake 40 minutes. Serves 12. This dish freezes very well.

BAKED ONION RINGS AND CHEESE

HICKORY BRIDGE FARM, Orrtanna, Pennsylvania
Dr. Jim and Nancy Jean Hammett have converted this lovely old farm, a few miles from Gettysburg, into a warm, comfortable inn where guests can enjoy fishing in the pond and long hikes in the woods and over the fields. Breakfast is served on the deck overlooking the brook or in the big farmhouse kitchen.

6 slices toast, buttered
3 cups onion rings,
   blanched
1/4 lb. American cheese,
   grated
1 egg, lightly beaten
1 cup milk
1 tsp. salt
1/8 tsp. freshly ground
   black pepper
1 tbsp. butter
paprika

Preheat oven to 375°. Place 3 slices of buttered toast in bottom of a medium-sized baking pan, then cover with a layer of 1 1/2 cup onions and another layer using half the cheese. Repeat. In a small bowl, combine egg, milk, salt and pepper. Pour over contents of baking pan. Dot with butter and sprinkle with paprika. Bake 30 to 35 minutes. Serves 4.

CHEESE CHARLOTTE

BARROWS HOUSE, Dorset, Vermont
Marilyn and Charlie Schubert make this one of New England's favorite stopping places—they create an atmosphere of friendly conviviality and personal hospitality. There are always many things to do here both summer and winter.

3 tbsp. butter
1 cup finely minced green
   onions
9 slices white bread,
   trimmed, lightly
      buttered, and cubed
1 1/2 lbs. sharp cheddar
   cheese, grated
1 1/2 tsp. salt
1/4 tsp. freshly ground
   black pepper
1/2 tsp. dry mustard
3 cups milk
1 4-oz. can hot green
   chilis, thinly sliced
dash Tabasco
6 eggs, lightly beaten

Grease a 2-quart ovenproof casserole. In a small saucepan, melt butter and sauté green onions until they are translucent. In the prepared casserole, arrange half the bread cubes; cover with half the grated cheese. Repeat layering procedure with remaining bread and cheese. In a medium-sized bowl, combine salt, pepper and dry mustard, then gradually pour in milk. Add sautéed green onions, sliced chilis, Tabasco, and lightly beaten eggs and mix well. Pour egg mixture over bread and cheese, cover and refrigerate several hours or overnight. Two hours before serving return to room temperature. Preheat oven to 350° and bake the Charlotte 1 hour or until it is firm and browned. Serves 6.

GROUND BEEF QUICHE

MAINSTAY INN, Cape May, New Jersey
For a truly Victorian experience in a seaside village, this is the place to stay. Beautifully and elegantly furnished, this Italianate villa is authentic Victoriana in every respect. Sue Carroll makes delicious breakfasts, too.

1/2 lb. lean ground beef
3 eggs
1/2 cup mayonnaise
1/2 cup milk
1/4 cup grated onion
salt
freshly ground black
   pepper
2 cups grated cheddar
   cheese
1 9" unbaked pie crust,
   see recipe in Pies

Preheat oven to 350°. Brown meat and drain. In a large bowl, blend eggs with mayonnaise, milk, onion, salt and pepper to taste, and cheese. Add ground beef and pour mixture into pie crust. Bake 40 minutes or until lightly browned. Serves 6 to 8.

QUICHE LORRAINE

NAUSET HOUSE, East Orleans, Massachusetts

What a pleasure it is to sit on the sunlit terrace of this Cape Cod bed-and-breakfast inn and enjoy this superb breakfast quiche. It's just a short stroll to Nauset Beach.

1/2 lb. cooked ham, diced
1 9" unbaked pie crust,
  see recipe in Pies
1/4 lb. grated Muenster or
  Gruyere cheese
3 eggs, beaten
2 cups light cream
1 tsp. salt
pinch pepper
pinch cayenne pepper

Preheat oven to 400°. Layer ham in unbaked pie crust, cover with cheese. Blend other ingredients. Pour over cheese and ham. Bake for 30 to 40 minutes. Yield: One 9" quiche.

CHICKEN HASH

TOWN FARMS INN, Middletown, Connecticut

This elegant riverside inn is a kissin' cousin of the Griswold Inn in Essex, Connecticut, which is just a few minutes away. Sometimes this hash is served to the accompaniment of a string trio!

2 cups cooked chopped
  chicken
1 cup light cream
4 tbsp. butter
3 tbsp. flour
2 cups milk
1 tsp. salt
3 egg yolks
1/4 tsp. grated onion
1/3 cup grated Parmesan
  or Swiss cheese

Preheat broiler. Simmer the chicken in the cream until the cream is reduced by one-half. Make a white sauce: in a saucepan melt 3 tablespoons of the butter, add the flour and stir with a wire whisk until blended. Bring 1 1/4 cups of the milk to a boil and add all at once to the butter-flour mixture, stirring vigorously with the whisk until the sauce is thickened and smooth. Add 1/2 cup of the white sauce to the chicken mixture, season with salt, stir in one egg yolk and set aside. Mix the remaining white sauce and the remaining slightly beaten egg yolks with a little of the hot sauce. Add the remaining milk and the grated onion and cook, stirring until thickened and smooth. Add the remaining butter and one tablespoon of the cheese. Place the reserved hash in an ovenproof dish and cover with the sauce. Sprinkle with the remaining cheese. Brown under a hot broiler. Serves 4.

CHEESE ENCHILADAS

RANCHO de los CABALLEROS, Wickenburg, Arizona

The happy patrons of this posh guest ranch in the high country of Arizona enjoy not only tennis, swimming, and horseback riding, but also golf on the first nine holes of a projected championship course.

12 corn tortillas
1 cup shortening, melted
1 lb. cheddar cheese, shredded
1 10-oz. can pitted black olives, chopped
1 medium onion, finely chopped
2 16-oz. cans enchilada sauce

Preheat oven to 350°. Soften the tortillas by quickly dipping them in the hot shortening. Combine cheese, chopped olives and onion. Roll cheese mixture in the softened tortillas, dividing the mixture evenly among them. In a flat pan line the tortillas and cover with enchilada sauce. Bake 25 minutes. Yield: 12 enchiladas.

CREPES FLORENTINE

BENBOW INN, Garberville, California

An English Tudor manse with overtones of 1920s Art Deco—dark wood panelling, a truly massive fireplace, oriental rugs—among the giant redwoods of northern California. Route 101 buses stop almost at the front door of this destination resort-inn.

FILLING:

4 cups milk
1/2 tsp. salt
1/2 tsp. white pepper
1/2 tsp. celery salt
1/2 bay leaf
pinch ground cloves
pinch freshly grated nutmeg
1/2 cup butter
5/8 cup all-purpose flour
8 slices bacon, chopped
1 cup chopped onion
1 tsp. Worcestershire sauce
1/2 cup dry white wine
1 10-oz. package frozen chopped spinach, cooked and drained
1/2 pt. sour cream

In the top of a double boiler, combine milk and seasonings. In a small saucepan, prepare a roux: melt butter and add flour. Cook, whisking constantly, until roux begins to "honeycomb." When the seasoned milk is hot, add the roux, whisking constantly as the mixture thickens. Stirring constantly, cook five minutes longer. Meanwhile, in a 10 to 12" skillet, cook bacon until crisp. Drain and discard bacon fat. Add onions, Worcestershire and white wine to the skillet with the bacon and cook until onions are translucent. Add bacon mixture to the prepared sauce. Then add spinach and sour cream and combine thoroughly. Keep filling warm while you prepare the crepes.

CREPES:

1 1/2 cups all-purpose
  flour
1 tsp. salt
2 tsp. baking powder
4 eggs
1 1/3 cups milk
2/3 cup water
1/4 cup butter, melted

In a large mixing bowl, thoroughly combine crepe ingredients. Grease a crepe pan or skillet, and spoon the batter thinly on its surface. Turn the crepe to cook briefly. Yield: Sixteen 5" crepes.

To assemble Crepes Florentine: Spoon 2 tablespoons of filling onto each crepe, roll, and top with more filling. Serve two crepes per portion. Serves 8.

TURKEY HASH WITH MUSTARD SAUCE

OLD DROVERS INN, Dover Plains, New York

Country chic is the best description for this handsome inn about two hours north of New York City, which boasts but three lodging rooms. Country hash never tasted like this before—it's their most famous entrée at lunch, and does very well at dinner, also.

NOTE: *The success of this recipe depends on the use of Idaho potatoes. Prepare potato well in advance, being careful not to overcook, chill thoroughly, unpeeled. Each hash portion is cooked individually and kept warm while remaining servings are prepared.*

HASH:

3 cups cooked dark turkey
  meat
1 cup cooked white turkey
  meat
1 cup boiled, peeled Idaho
  potato
1/4 cup clarified butter

Finely chop turkey and chilled potato and mix well in large mixing bowl. Preheat oven to 225°. In a large mixing bowl, combine all ingredients except butter. In a 5" skillet, for each serving, bring 1 tablespoon of the clarified butter almost to the smoking point. Add 1 1/4 cups of the hash to the skillet and cook 4 to 5 minutes, or until hash begins to pull away from sides of the skillet and is golden brown. Transfer, bottom side up, to a warmed plate. Place in preheated oven while you prepare remaining portions. Serves 4.

MUSTARD SAUCE:

1 1/2 cups chicken stock
1/4 cup beef stock
1 tbsp. butter
1 tbsp. flour
1/4 cup Gulden's mustard
1 tbsp. Coleman's dry
  mustard
salt
freshly ground black
  pepper

Heat chicken and beef stock. In a small saucepan, make a roux, melting the butter and whisking in the flour. Cook 2 to 3 minutes. When stock is just below boiling, add the roux, whisking constantly and season with mustards, salt and pepper to taste. Simmer until sauce is cooked through. To serve, spoon sauce over individual portions of Turkey Hash.

CHICKEN CHEESE CASSEROLE

BEAUMONT INN, Harrodsburg, Kentucky

This antebellum inn in the heart of the bluegrass country is famous for its ham dishes, but here is a chicken dish that is bound to attract many a palate. Although proportions given would provide a fine entrée for a buffet dinner party, this casserole freezes very well for later, smaller servings.

1 5-lb. hen cooked,
   skinned and diced
5 oz. spaghetti
chicken stock
1 lb. sharp cheese, grated
1 16-oz. can mushrooms
1 large onion, finely
   chopped
1 green pepper, diced
1 stalk celery, diced
1 qt. white sauce,
   see Sauces
8 pieces melba toast,
   crumbled
4 tbsp. melted butter

Cook spaghetti in chicken stock and drain. Preheat oven to 350°. Combine all ingredients, except crumbled toast and melted butter, which should be combined separately. Place chicken and spaghetti mixture in 6 oz. individual casserole dishes and sprinkle each with crumbled toast, or use 1 large casserole dish, if preferred. Bake in oven until casserole bubbles. Serves 21.

CRABMEAT AND AVOCADO QUICHE

SHERWOOD INN, Skaneateles, New York

Guests at this Finger Lakes Inn can enjoy dinner while looking out over the delightful scenery of Lake Owasco. This crabmeat and avocado quiche is an easy-to-make dish with a different flavor.

1 1/2 cups grated Swiss
   cheese
1 baked 9" pie crust, see
   recipe in Pies
1/2 lb. crabmeat
3 tbsp. butter
1 avocado, cubed
2 tsp. Dijon-type mustard
2 tsp. lemon juice
6 large egg yolks
2 cups heavy cream
1 cup milk
1 1/4 tsp. white pepper
1/2 tsp. freshly grated
   nutmeg
1 1/4 tsp. salt

Preheat the oven to 425°. Place cheese in bottom of pie crust. Sauté crabmeat in butter, remove from the skillet and drain on paper towels. Combine avocado, mustard and lemon juice. Mix avocado and crabmeat and place over Swiss cheese. In a medium-sized bowl gently mix the egg yolks. In a separate bowl combine cream and milk and pour into egg yolks. Season with white pepper, nutmeg and salt. Pour the egg mixture over the crabmeat and avocado. Bake at 425° for ten minutes, reduce heat to 325° and continue to bake for an additional 40 minutes, or until a silver knife inserted into center of quiche comes out clean. Yield: One 9" quiche.

BREADS

STAFFORD'S IN THE FIELD

ROBERT MORRIS INN

ST. GEMME BEAUVAIS INN

LEMON PUFFS

STAFFORD'S IN THE FIELD, Chocorua, New Hampshire

This is the inn at "the end of the road" in one of New Hampshire's picturesque villages. Ramona Stafford is well-known for her truly gourmet cooking. This recipe is from her own cookbook-in-preparation.

1/2 cup hot water
1 package active dry yeast
5 eggs, beaten
2 tbsp. powdered milk
1/4 cup melted butter
1/3 cup sugar, plus sugar
   for topping
finely grated rind of one
   lemon
1/2 tsp. salt
4 1/2 cups flour
1 egg yolk, beaten
finely chopped walnuts

Combine water and yeast and set aside to dissolve. In a large mixing bowl, combine eggs, powdered milk, melted butter, 1/3 cup of the sugar, lemon rind, and salt. Add dissolved yeast and mix well. Stir in flour. Allow dough to rise in a bowl until it is doubled in volume. Punch down, remove from bowl and knead lightly on floured board. Dough will be smooth and soft. Place in a clean bowl and set aside to rise again until doubled in volume. Punch down again and knead out the bubbles. Preheat oven to 350°. Grease two baking sheets. Shape dough into 1" balls and place them 1" apart on prepared baking sheets. Brush the tops with egg yolk, and sprinkle with sugar and finely chopped walnuts. Bake 15 minutes and serve at once. Yield: 30 rolls.

CRANBERRY MUFFINS

ROBERT MORRIS INN, Oxford, Maryland

Best reached by the oldest (and probably smallest) car ferry in the country, this handsome early 18th-century home has original beams, panels, floors, and fireplace. It is in the midst of unspoiled Chesapeake Bay waterways and countryside. This is one of the Robert Morris's favorite Christmas recipes.

1 cup sifted flour
1/2 cup sugar
3/4 tsp. baking powder
1/4 tsp. baking soda
1/2 tsp. salt
2 tbsp. butter
3/8 cup orange juice, plus
   1/2 tsp. grated orange
   peel
1 egg, beaten
1/2 cup coarsely chopped
   fresh cranberries
1/4 cup chopped nuts

Preheat oven to 350°. Grease two 12-cup muffin tins. In a large mixing bowl, sift together dry ingredients. Cut in butter. Combine juice, orange peel, and egg. Add to dry ingredients, mixing only enough to moisten. Fold in cranberries and nuts. Transfer to prepared muffin tins. Bake 15 minutes. Cool and wrap overnight. Warm and serve next day. Yield: 24 muffins.

FRENCH CRULLERS

ST. GEMME BEAUVAIS INN, Ste. Genevieve, Missouri
The French heritage of Ste. Genevieve, a village on the Mississippi River, is apparent in the buildings, many of which were built before 1800. The inn is really a showcase for the village with its handsome wrought iron fence. Innkeepers Frankye and Boats Donze have furnished it with carved furniture, marble-top dressers, floral wallpapers, and bright carpets, and their breakfasts and lunches feature tasty specialties of all kinds.

4 cups flour
4 tsp. baking powder
1/2 tsp. salt
1/4 tsp. freshly grated
  nutmeg
1 1/2 cups sugar
3 eggs, beaten
1 tsp. vanilla extract
6 tbsp. butter, softened
1 cup milk
fat for deep frying
confectioners sugar

Sift flour. Add baking powder, salt and nutmeg then sift the dry ingredients 3 more times. In a large mixing bowl add the sugar to the beaten eggs and beat until lemon yellow in color. Beat in the vanilla and the butter. Alternately add the dry ingredients and the milk to the egg mixture, mixing well after each addition.

Lightly knead the dough on a floured board. Roll out to 1/3-inch thickness. Cut with doughnut cutter or knife and deep fry until golden brown, turning frequently. Drain on unglazed paper and sprinkle with powdered sugar. Serve hot. Yield: About 2 dozen doughnuts.

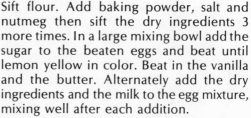

GUMDROP BREAD

OUTLOOK LODGE, Green Mountain Falls, Colorado
Nostalgia is the theme at this bed-and-breakfast rustic lodge on the slopes of Pike's Peak. Informal gatherings and old-fashioned entertainments, and breakfasts with delicious homemade breads make this a friendly, fun place to stay.

3 cups flour
3/4 cup sugar
3 1/2 tsp. baking powder
1 tsp. salt
1 1/2 cups milk
1 egg, beaten
2 tbsp. vegetable oil
3/4 cup chopped
  gumdrops
1/2 cup chopped walnuts

Preheat oven to 350°. Grease and flour a 9x5x3" loaf pan. In a large mixing bowl, combine flour, sugar, baking powder, and salt. In a separate bowl, mix together milk, egg, and oil. Add egg mixture to dry ingredients, stirring only until batter is moistened. Fold in gumdrops and nuts. Pour batter into prepared pan and bake 1 hour. Unmold immediately. Yield: One 9x5x3" loaf.

OUTLOOK LODGE

GREENVILLE ARMS

PHILBROOK FARM

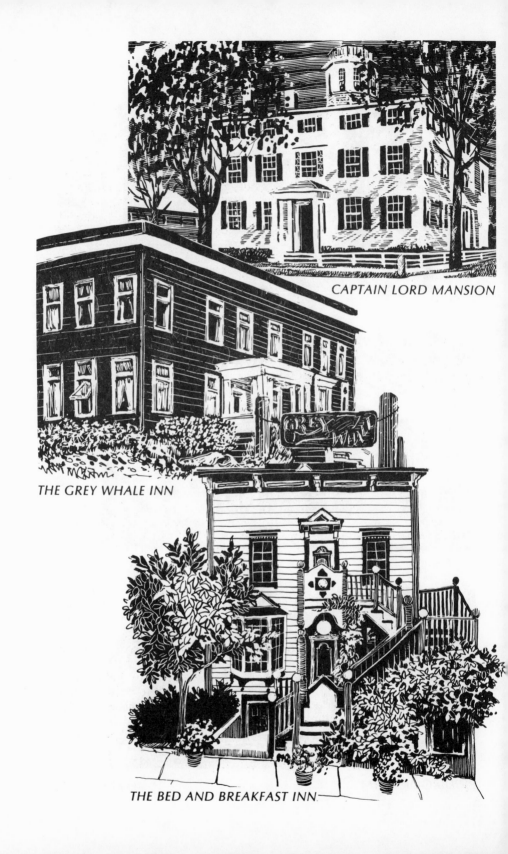

CAPTAIN LORD MANSION

THE GREY WHALE INN

THE BED AND BREAKFAST INN

ST. TIMOTHY'S COFFEECAKE

THE GREY WHALE INN, Fort Bragg, California

This weatherbeaten inn, which was formerly a hospital, is located on northern California's Mendocino coast. Lodgings include breakfast and may very often include this recipe which we are pleased to present.

1 cup butter, softened
2 cups sugar
1/2 tsp. vanilla extract
2 eggs
2 cups flour
1 tsp. baking powder
1/4 tsp. salt
1 tsp. ground cinnamon
1/2 cup golden raisins
1 cup chopped nuts
1 cup sour cream
**cinnamon sugar for
    topping**

Preheat oven to 350°. Grease and flour a 3-quart Bundt cake mold. In a large mixing bowl, cream butter until fluffy, then gradually add sugar and continue to cream the mixture. Add vanilla. Add eggs one at a time, beating well after each addition. Sift together flour, baking powder, salt, and cinnamon. To the sifted ingredients, add the raisins and nuts, stirring to coat them thoroughly. Add the sifted dry ingredients to the butter cream alternately with the sour cream and blend well. Pour into prepared Bundt cake mold. Sprinkle with cinnamon sugar. Bake 1 hour or until a toothpick inserted in center of cake comes out clean. Cool at least 1 hour before unmolding. Yield: One 10" coffeecake.

ZUCCHINI BREAD

CAPTAIN LORD MANSION, Kennebunkport, Maine

Guests at the CLM are transported into an elegant era of the nineteenth century. It is a mansion of over thirty-five rooms of many descriptions and a cupola where one can hide away in seclusion and read a book. Many guests rhapsodize about Bev's breakfasts—and particularly her Zucchini Bread which, she tells me, is different from most.

3 eggs
2 1/2 cups sugar
1 cup vegetable oil
2 cups finely diced zucchini
1 tsp. vanilla extract
3 cups flour
3 tsp. ground cinnamon
1 tsp. salt
1 tsp. baking soda
1 1/2 tsp. baking powder
1 cup raisins

Preheat oven to 350°. Grease and flour two 9x5x3" loaf pans. In a large mixing bowl, beat eggs until they are light and fluffy and lemon-colored. Add sugar and oil and combine thoroughly. Fold in zucchini and vanilla. Sift together dry ingredients and fold them into the egg mixture along with the raisins. Pour batter into prepared loaf pans and bake 1 hour or until a toothpick inserted into the center of each loaf comes out clean. Yield: Two 9x5x3" loaves of bread.

LONESOME PINE CORNCAKE

BOONE TAVERN HOTEL, Berea, Kentucky
Most of the dishes served at this central Kentucky hotel are from cookbooks written by former innkeeper Dick Hougen, who said, "I'd classify our food as southern gourmet rather than southern fried." The town is also the site of Berea College, a most unique institution of higher learning, which provides the young people of Appalachia with the opportunity of becoming acquainted with the Humanities, and also furthers their natural skills in the mountain crafts identified with the southern highlands.

1/2 cup sifted flour
2 cups white cornmeal
3 tsp. baking powder
1/2 tsp. salt
1/2 cup milk
2 eggs, beaten
1/2 tsp. baking soda
1 1/2 cups buttermilk
5 tbsp. lard, melted, plus
   lard for greasing baking
   pan

Preheat oven to 475°. In a large mixing bowl, sift together flour, cornmeal, baking powder and salt. In a separate bowl, combine milk and beaten eggs, add them to the dry ingredients and mix well. In another bowl, combine baking soda and buttermilk, add to cornmeal batter and mix well. Finally, add melted lard and mix batter until ingredients are thoroughly combined. Heat a 9x13" baking pan in the oven, then grease the pan well with lard. Pour batter into hot pan and bake 30 minutes. Yield: 12 to 18 squares. Also good for use in stuffings.

DUTCH BABIES

HEARTHSTONE INN, Colorado Springs, Colorado
With its delightful Victorian atmosphere, this restored historical mansion near the heart of the city offers wonderful breakfasts to its guests, along with a crackling fire on cold mornings. This recipe for a sort of puffy pancake, somewhat like a popover, always makes a big hit with the guests.

Note: To make Dutch Babies, it is important to use a shallow pan—not over 3" deep; size and shape of pan are not important. Measure the quart volume of the pan with water. Proportion of ingredients is given below for a representative variety of pan sizes.

PAN SIZE	BUTTER	EGGS	MILK/FLOUR
2-3 qts.	1/4 cup	3	3/4 cup each
3-4 qts.	1/3 cup	4	1 cup each
4-4 1/2 qts.	1/2 cup	5	1 1/4 cup each
4 1/2-5 qts.	1/2 cup	6	1 1/2 cup each

Preheat oven to 425°. Place butter in pan and heat in oven until butter is melted. Meanwhile in a blender, prepare batter: At high speed, beat eggs well for one minute. With the blender motor running, pour in milk, then gradually add flour. Blend an additional 30 seconds. Remove pan from oven and pour batter onto melted butter. Return to oven and bake 30 to 40 minutes or until the Dutch Babies are puffy and browned. Dutch babies should be served piping hot with any of the following: freshly grated nutmeg, honey or maple syrup, strawberries, or a topping of lemon juice and confectioners sugar. Serves 4.

MARILY'S "STICKY BUNS"

THE BED AND BREAKFAST INN, San Francisco, California
In the middle of San Francisco on a little English "mews" stands this delightfully Victorian inn. The lodging rooms have such names as Covent Garden, Chelsea, and Kensington Garden, and they are all different with charming decorative touches, such as old-fashioned ceiling fans, all varieties of beds—from Victorian carved headboards to shiny brass bedsteads—baskets of fruit, and flowers everywhere.

1/2 cup pecans
1/2 cup butter
1 cup firmly packed light
    brown sugar
2 tbsp. water
2 8-oz. tubes crescent
    dinner rolls
1/2 cup raisins
1 tsp. ground cinnamon

Preheat oven to 350°. Grease a 3-quart Bundt pan. Sprinkle 1/4 cup of the pecans in the bottom of the Bundt pan. In a small saucepan, combine the butter, light brown sugar, water, and remaining 1/4 cup of pecans. Bring the mixture to a boil and simmer one minute. Pour 1/2 of the brown sugar mixture over the pecans in the bottom of the Bundt pan. Cut the contents of each tube of crescent rolls into eight slices. Arrange the contents of one tube of rolls over the brown sugar mixture in the pan. Sprinkle with 1/4 cup of raisins and 1/2 teaspoon of the cinnamon. Spoon remaining sugar mixture over the raisins and cinnamon. Place the remaining dough slices so that they overlap the lower slices and are not directly one on top of the other. Sprinkle the remaining raisins and cinnamon over the dough. Bake 25 minutes. Cool on a rack for 10 minutes, then invert the Bundt pan to unmold the sticky buns. Yield: 16 Sticky Buns.

CLOUD BISCUITS

GREENVILLE ARMS, Greenville, New York

Greenville Arms is a Victorian country home with several interesting porches cupolas, gables, and corners. Well-shaded with tall trees and beautifully landscaped with bushes and shrubs, it's been a way of life for many years for innkeeper Ruth Stevens who is too self-effacing to concede she is one of the best cooks in Greene County.

2 cups sifted flour
1 tbsp. sugar
4 tsp. baking powder
1/2 tsp. salt
1/2 cup shortenting
1 egg, beaten
2/3 cup milk

Preheat oven to 450°. Into a large mixing bowl, sift together dry ingredients, cut in shortening until mixture resembles coarse crumbs. In a small bowl, combine egg and milk, then add to flour mixture all at once. Stir until blended. Turn out on lightly floured surface. Knead gently with heel of hand 20 strokes. Roll dough to 3/4-inch thickness. Dip 2-inch biscuit cutter in flour; cut straight down through dough, do not twist cutter. Place circles on ungreased baking sheet (3/4 inch apart for crusty biscuits, close together for soft sides). Bake 10 to 14 minutes or until golden brown. Yield: 8 large biscuits.

DARK BREAD

PHILBROOK FARM, Shelburne, New Hampshire

This farmhouse-inn has been run by the same family since the late 1800s, and is an outstanding example of a fast-disappearing type of accommodation. Innkeeper-sisters Connie Leger and Nancy Philbrook personify the good humor to be found in New Hampshire's White Mountains. Three meals are served every day, accompanied by home-baked bread like this. It's small wonder that many of the guests return year after year.

2 cups all purpose flour
2 tsp. baking soda
1 tsp. salt
1 1/2 cups graham flour
1/2 cup firmly packed
brown sugar
1/2 cup dark molasses
2 cups sour milk or
buttermilk

Preheat oven to 350°. Grease and flour one 9x5x3" loaf pan. Into a large bowl, sift together all purpose flour, baking soda, and salt. Add remaining ingredients to sifted dry ingredients and combine thoroughly. Transfer dough to prepared loaf pan and bake 1 hour or until a toothpick inserted into center of bread comes out clean. Yield: One 9x5x3" loaf dark bread. Raisins or dates may be added to the batter if desired.

CAKES

ASA RANSOM HOUSE

1740 HOUSE

PILGRIM'S INN

PUMPKIN CAKE ROLL

ASA RANSOM HOUSE, Clarence, New York

Bob and Judy Lenz use only natural ingredients for all of their menu items at this inn in a restored Victorian house in western New York State. The Pumpkin Cake Roll is one of the favorites on their menu.

1/2 cup sugar
3 eggs
2/3 cup canned pumpkin
1 tsp. lemon juice
1/2 cup wheat flour
1/4 cup flour
1 tsp. baking powder
2 tsp. ground cinnamon
1 tsp. ground ginger
1/2 tsp. freshly grated
  nutmeg

Preheat oven to 375°. Grease a 10x15" baking pan. In a large mixing bowl beat eggs until very thick. Gradually beat the sugar into the eggs. Stir in the pumpkin and lemon juice. Sift together the dry ingredients, then fold them into the pumpkin mixture. Pour the batter into the prepared pan and bake 15 minutes. Transfer cake to a towel; roll towel and cake together jelly roll fashion; cool; unroll.

FILLING:

3 oz. cream cheese,
  softened
1/2 cup heavy cream,
  whipped
1/2 cup confectioners
  sugar
4 tbsp. butter, softened
1/2 tsp. vanilla extract

Beat all ingredients together until smooth.

To assemble the Pumpkin Cake Roll, place the cake on waxed paper, spread the filling on the cake, roll jelly roll fashion, and chill. Serves 8 to 10.

FRESH APPLE CAKE

GRAVES MOUNTAIN LODGE, Syria, Virginia

Located in the beautiful Blue Ridge Mountains, this inn is set in the middle of thousands of acres of its own fruit orchards. Meals are served family-style at long tables. This is just one of the many apple dishes on the menu.

2 cups sugar
1 cup vegetable oil
2 eggs
2 1/2 cups flour
1 tsp. baking soda
1 tsp. baking powder
1 tsp. ground cinnamon
1 tsp. salt
1/4 tsp. freshly grated
  nutmeg
3 cups, peeled, chopped
  apples
1 6-oz. package
  butterscotch chips

Preheat oven to 350°. Grease an 8x13" baking pan. Blend together the sugar and oil and gradually beat in the eggs. Sift together the dry ingredients. Add them alternately with the apples to the egg mixture, mixing well. Pour the batter into prepared pan. Cover with the butterscotch chips. Bake 45 minutes. Yield: One 8x13" cake.

JOYOUS STRAWBERRY GRANITA CAKE

PILGRIM'S INN, Deer Isle, Maine

This historic Maine seacoast inn with its gambrel roof was floated over to Deer Isle from the mainland by Squire Haskell in 1793. Here is one of innkeeper Elli Pavloff's delightful concoctions. She cautions you to slice this cake only after your guests have seen your gorgeous creation.

GRANITA:

2 cups frozen, unsweetened, whole strawberries
grated rind of one orange
3 tbsp. orange juice
1 tbsp. Cointreau or Triple Sec

To make the Granita, combine the frozen strawberries, orange rind, orange juice, and Cointreau. Blend until thick and set aside in freezer.

1 homemade pound cake (or packaged frozen cake)
1 qt. vanilla ice cream
whole, fresh strawberries or mint leaves
whipped cream

With a bread knife, cut a 3/4" slice from the top of the pound cake. Set aside. Scoop out enough of the inside of the cake to hold 1 1/2 cup of Granita. Reserving 1/2 cup of the Granita, fill the hollow with the strawberry mixture. Replace top of the cake. Ice cake with 1/2" layer of vanilla ice cream, making a ridge around the edge of the icing. Spread the reserved 1/2 cup of Granita in this depression. Garnish with whole, fresh strawberries or mint leaves, and serve with whipped cream, if desired.

GATEAU CHRISTINA

CHALET SUZANNE, Lake Wales, Florida

"Phantasmagoric" is the only word for this delightful inn with its conglomeration of little cottages, lodges, and chalets in a collection of styles that could be Oriental, Persian, Bavarian, Swiss, or chocolate layer cake. The food is superb.

MERINGUE:

4 egg whites
1 1/2 cups sugar
1/3 cup blanched ground almonds

Preheat oven to 250°. Cut four rounds of aluminum foil about 8" in diameter. Lightly grease foil rounds. Whip egg whites until stiff, gradually adding sugar and ground almonds as eggs begin to hold their shape. Spread meringue on foil rounds with rubber spatuala. Transfer rounds to a baking sheet and bake 15 minutes, or until meringue is dry. Carefully turn meringues over and bake 5 additional minutes. Baking time will vary depending on atmospherical humidity and individual oven.

CHOCOLATE FILLING:

2 egg whites
1/2 cup sugar
2 tbsp. sweetened cocoa
1 cup butter, softened
4 oz. semisweet chocolate,
  melted

In the top of a double boiler, over hot, not boiling, water, beat egg whites until foamy. Gradually add and whisk: sugar, cocoa, softened butter and melted chocolate. Beat until thick and creamy, then remove from heat. Cool.

To assemble the gateau: Reserve some chocolate filling for icing. Place the best meringue layer on bottom, spread with chocolate. Top with another meringue circle, pressing down lightly to make layers fit together well. Spread with chocolate. Repeat procedure until all meringue circles are used. Carefully top with reserved filling. Refrigerate the gateau at least 24 hours. Gateau keeps well under refrigeration. It may be made with smaller meringue circles and stored in tin boxes for Christmas gifts. Yield: One 4-layered 8" gateau.

TIA MARIA CAKE

1740 HOUSE, Lumberville, Pennsylvania
In this 18th-century farmhouse on the banks of the Delaware River, where every room has a balcony overlooking the river, Harry Nessler has established a tradition of attention to detail in furnishings, meals, and service. Here's an example of the kind of delightful fare he offers.

6 eggs, separated, plus 1
  whole egg
3/4 cup sugar
1 cup ground walnuts
1/3 cup ground Ritz
  cracker crumbs
2 cups heavy cream
4 tbsp. Tia Maria
2 squares semisweet
  chocolate, shaved

Preheat oven to 350°. Lightly grease two 9" layer cake pans and line with waxed paper. In a medium-sized bowl beat the whole egg and the egg yolks with sugar until lemon colored and foamy. Add ground walnuts and cracker crumbs. In a large bowl beat egg whites until stiff peaks are formed. Gradually fold egg yolk mixture into egg whites. Pour equal amounts of mixture into the cake pans. Bake for 20 minutes, or until surface springs back when gently pressed. Let cool in pans on wire rack. Whip the cream and Tia Maria. Fill and frost the cake with the whipped cream mixture. Sprinkle the top and sides with the chocolate shavings. Yield: One 2-layered 9" cake.

CHOCOLATE PEPPERMINT LAYER CAKE

KEDRON VALLEY INN, South Woodstock, Vermont

Paul and Barbara Kendall and their sons Chip and Dane are proud of the fact that there have been Kendalls in the Kedron Valley for seven generations. This is in the center of Vermont's horse country in summer, and excellent cross-country skiing in the winter.

CAKE:

2 1/4 cups sifted cake flour
2 tsp. baking soda
1/2 tsp. salt
1/2 tsp. ground cinnamon
1/2 cup butter
1 1-lb. box firmly packed brown sugar
3 eggs
3 1-oz. squares unsweetened chocolate, melted
1/2 cup sour milk or buttermilk
1 tsp. vanilla extract
1 cup boiling water

Preheat oven to 350°. Grease bottoms and sides of two 10x2" layer cake pans. Flour lightly. Sift cake flour, measure carefully and sift again with soda, salt, and cinnamon. Cream butter and sugar until very light and airy adding only a small amount of sugar to the batter at a time. Add eggs one at a time beating well after each addition. Add chocolate to batter and beat some more. Sift about 1/3 of flour mixture into batter, stir well, add 1/3 of the buttermilk or sour milk and stir slightly, add another 1/3 of flour and milk and repeat adding flour last. Add vanilla, then boiling water and mix quickly. Pour into prepared pans. Batter will be thin. Bake 35 to 40 minutes. Place pans on wire rack to cool 5 minutes. Loosen around edges and remove from pans. Cool layers completely before icing. May also be baked in 3 eight-inch layers or in cupcake pans. Freezes very well.

FILLING:

1/2 cup sugar
3 tbsp. light cream
1 tbsp. butter
1 egg yolk
pinch of salt
1 1-oz. square unsweetened chocolate
1/2 tsp. peppermint extract

In a small saucepan combine sugar, light cream, butter, egg yolk, salt, and chocolate. Heat over low flame stirring constantly until mixture comes to a boil and is smooth and thick. Add 1/2 tsp. peppermint extract and beat for about 1 minute. Pour onto bottom layer of cake and spread to the edge of cake. Set for a few minutes before adding top layer. Frost with seven-minute icing.

ICING:

1/3 cup water
1 tbsp. light corn syrup
1 1/2 cups sugar
2 egg whites
1/4 tsp. salt

In the top of a double boiler combine water, corn syrup, sugar, egg whites, and salt. Place over hot water and beat with electric mixer until stiff enough to allow you to pull the beater from the icing and

5 drops green or red food
  coloring
1 tsp. peppermint extract
1 1/2 oz. unsweetened
  chocolate, melted with
  1 tbsp. butter

leave a hole. Remove from heat. Add 5 drops of food coloring and peppermint extract. Continue beating until almost cold. Spread on sides and top of cake. Immediately dribble with melted chocolate and butter mixture. Yield: One 2-layered 10" cake.

CHOCOLATE CAKE

INN AT SAWMILL FARM, West Dover, Vermont
Called a model for all country inns, this resort-inn offers luxurious accommodations and delicious meals along with unlimited possibilities for diversion. Ione Williams's desserts are out of this world, and I'm sure her chocolate cake is no exception.

CAKE:

1 cup unsweetened cocoa
2 cups boiling water
2 2/3 cups sifted cake flour
2 tsp. baking soda
1/2 tsp. salt
1/2 tsp. baking powder
1 cup butter, softened
2 1/2 cups sugar
4 eggs
1 1/2 tsp. vanilla extract

Preheat oven to 350°. Grease and flour three 9x1 1/2" layer cake pans. Whisk together cocoa and boiling water. Cool. Meanwhile, sift together flour, soda, salt, and baking powder. In a large bowl and at high speed on an electric mixer, beat 5 minutes, or until light: butter, sugar, eggs, and vanilla. At low speed, alternately beat in flour and cocoa mixtures, beginning and ending with flour. Do not overbeat. Divide batter evenly among prepared cake pans and bake 25 to 30 minutes or until a toothpick inserted into center of cake comes out clean. Cool on racks.

FILLING:

1 cup heavy cream
1/4 cup confectioners
  sugar
1 tsp. vanilla extract

In a medium-sized mixing bowl, whip heavy cream until it begins to hold its shape. As you continue whipping, gradually sift in confectioners sugar, then add vanilla. Spread filling evenly between cooled layers of cake and refrigerate at least 2 hours before frosting.

FROSTING:

6 oz. chocolate chips
1/4 cup light cream
1 cup butter
2 1/2 cups confectioners
  sugar

In a heavy saucepan, combine chocolate chips, light cream, and butter. Stir and cook over medium heat until smooth. Remove from heat and place saucepan in a bowl with ice. Beat in confectioners sugar until frosting holds its shape. Frost the cake and refrigerate at least 1 hour. Yield: One 3-layered 9" cake.

THORNOBY TEA TORTE

PEIRSON PLACE, Richmond, Massachusetts

Many guests return to this bed-and-breakfast inn year after year for the shaded quiet of the woodland walks, as well as the proximity to Tanglewood, Jacob's Pillow, the Berkshire Playhouse, and Williamstown. Afternoon teas are friendly and fun. Here's a delectable concoction to enhance the fanciest of teas.

MERINGUE:

3/4 cup egg whites (about
   6 eggs) at room
   temperature
1/4 tsp. salt
1/4 tsp. cream of tartar
1 3/4 cup sugar
1 1/2 tsp. vanilla extract
1 1/2 cup ground pecans

Preheat the oven to 225°. Draw 10" circles on three pieces of cooking parchment and place on three baking sheets. Make sure all utensils are free from grease. In the large bowl of an electric mixer, at low speed, beat egg whites until foamy. Add salt and cream of tartar and beat at medium speed until egg whites hold their shape and form soft peaks. Beat in 1 cup of the sugar, 1/4 cup at a time. Continue to beat at high speed until sugar is completely dissolved. Fold in remaining 3/4 cup of sugar, vanilla, and ground pecans, using 1/4 cup of sugar and 1/2 cup of pecans at a time. Fit a pastry bag with a 1/2" plain tip and fill with meringue. To fill each circle of parchment paper, use a spiral motion, starting at the edge of each circle and working towards its center. Smooth each circle with a spatula. Place the baking sheets on upper and middle racks of oven; immediately reduce oven temperature to 200°. Bake 1 hour or until meringues slide when touched gently. Transfer from the baking sheets and parchment paper to racks to cool. Meanwhile prepare filling.

FILLING:

3 1/2 cups sugar
2 cups strong coffee
1 1/2 cups butter, softened,
   plus 1/2 cup butter that
   may be required for
   syrup
confectioners sugar

In a large saucepan, combine sugar and coffee and cook over medium heat until mixture reaches 232° on a candy thermometer. Use the 1/2 cup butter if required to keep syrup from boiling over. Remove from heat and cool syrup until it is just warm. At high speed on an electric mixer beat the 1 1/2 cups softened butter until it is light and fluffy. At medium speed, gradually pour in syrup. If mixture is too thin, refrigerate 20 minutes and beat again. It should be the consistency of whipped cream.

To assemble the torte: Place one layer of meringue on a serving plate. Spread 1/4 of the filling on meringue. Repeat until you have used all layers. Use remaining filling to ice sides of torte. Sprinkle top with confectioners sugar. Allow torte to set two hours before serving. If torte is not to be served the same day, refrigerate it, removing it from the refrigerator one hour before serving. Yield: One 3-layered 10" torte.

BLUEBERRY CAKE

ROCKHOUSE MOUNTAIN FARM, Eaton Center, New Hampshire
Guest-friends have been returning to this farm-inn for as many as thirty years. Complete with farm animals, horses, and a hay-filled barn, as well as a lake and many other recreational possibilities, this is a delightful vacation place for children and adults alike.

3 tbsp. shortening
1 cup sugar, plus sugar for
   sprinkling on cake
1 egg
1 3/4 cups flour
2 tsp. baking powder
1 tsp. salt
1 tsp. ground cinnamon
3/4 cup milk
1 to 1 1/2 cups fresh or
   frozen blueberries

Preheat oven to 375°. In a large mixing bowl, cream shortening and sugar until they are light and fluffy. Add egg. Reserving some flour to coat the blueberries before folding into the batter, combine and sift the dry ingredients and add to the creamed mixture alternately with the milk. Fold the floured blueberries into the batter. Transfer to a 9"-square cake pan. Sprinkle top generously with sugar before baking 30 minutes. Serve warm with sauce. Yield: 9 large or 12 small pieces.

SAUCE FOR BLUEBERRY CAKE:

1 cup sugar
3 tbsp. flour
3 tbsp. cold water
1 cup boiling water
1 egg yolk, lightly beaten
2 tsp. vanilla extract

In a small saucepan, combine sugar, flour, and cold water to make a paste. Slowly add boiling water and boil 10 minutes until thickened. Add some hot mixture to egg yolk before combining all ingredients, except vanilla. Cook 5 minutes longer. Add vanilla.

THE JOHN HANCOCK INN

FAIRFIELD INN

ROCKHOUSE MOUNTAIN FARM

CHEESECAKE DOUCETTE

THE JOHN HANCOCK INN, Hancock, New Hampshire

The famous American patriot for whom this inn is named, never visited the village, but Glynn and Pat Wells and their children have been here since the early 1970s. It's been a pleasure for me not only to record their progress, but to enjoy many a hearty meal and a night's rest at this secluded village inn in southern New Hampshire.

4 eggs
1 cup sugar, plus 2 tbsp.
  sugar
2 1/2 tsp. vanilla extract
3 8-oz. packages cream
  cheese, softened
1 graham cracker crust, see
  recipe in Pies
1 pt. sour cream

Place graham cracker crust in a 9" spring-form pan. Preheat oven to 350°. At moderate speed, beat together for 20 minutes eggs, 1 cup of the sugar, 1 1/2 teaspoon vanilla, and cream cheese. Pour mixture into crust and bake 30 minutes. Cool 15 minutes. Combine sour cream, remaining 2 tablespoons sugar, and remaining teaspoon vanilla. Pour over baked and cooled filled crust. Return to oven for 10 minutes. Chill at least 24 hours before serving. Serve topped with strawberries, Melba sauce, or another sauce of your choice. Yield: One 9" cheesecake.

SHOO FLY CAKE

FAIRFIELD INN, Fairfield, Pennsylvania

Built in 1755, this inn-restaurant was once a stagecoach stop on the Great Road from York to Hagerstown. The ham and bean soup that the townswomen served General Lee's starving confederate soldiers after the Battle of Gettysburg is one of the Fairfield Inn's specialties today. The big draw here is the great country-style cooking.

4 cups flour
2 cups firmly packed
  brown sugar
pinch salt
3/4 cup vegetable oil
1 cup dark molasses
1 tsp. baking soda
2 1/4 cups boiling water
whipped cream for
  topping

Preheat oven to 350°. Grease a 9x13" baking pan. In a large bowl, combine flour, brown sugar, salt and vegetable oil to make a crumbly mixture. Set aside 1 1/2 cups of the crumbs. In another bowl, mix molasses, baking soda, and boiling water. Gradually combine with remaining crumbs. Pour batter into prepared pan. Sprinkle reserved 1 1/2 cups of crumbs over top of cake. Bake at 350° for 15 minutes. Reduce oven temperature to 300° and bake an additional 30 minutes. Serve warm, topped with whipped cream. Yield: One 9x13" cake.

CINNAMON FLIP

SWORDGATE INN, Charleston, South Carolina
Well-preserved, quiet elegance typifies this beautifully furnished, stately old Charleston mansion. Its grand ballroom is included in the historic tours of the town. This is a time-honored recipe from a book of Charleston "receipts."

2 tbsp. shortening
1 cup sugar
1 cup milk
1 egg
1 1/2 cups flour, plus
  additional flour for
  sprinkling on top of flip
2 tsp. baking powder
3 tbsp. brown sugar
2 tsp. butter
1/2 tsp. ground cinnamon

Preheat oven to 350°. Grease a 9x13" baking pan. Cream shortening until it is light and fluffy, gradually add sugar and continue creaming. Add milk, egg, flour, and baking powder and beat until all the ingredients are thoroughly combined. Pour batter into prepared baking pan, smoothing the top with a spatula. Sift a sprinkling of flour over the flip; then sprinkle with brown sugar, dot with butter, and sprinkle with cinnamon. Bake 40 minutes. Serve hot or cold. Serves 12 to 14.

PINEAPPLE ICEBOX CAKE

VILLAGE INN, Lenox, Massachusetts
In the middle of the charming Colonial village of Lenox, this inn has been operating since the early 1800s, and the building itself dates back to the American Revolution. All of the cultural and recreational attractions of the Berkshires are within easy distance.

1 cup butter, softened
3 cups confectioners sugar
4 eggs
1 lb. vanilla wafers
1 pt. heavy cream
2 tbsp. sugar
2 8-oz. cans crushed
  pineapple, drained

Line an 8"-square pan with waxed paper. In a medium-sized mixing bowl, cream together butter and confectioners sugar. Add eggs one at a time, beating well after each addition. Roll vanilla wafers fine, place the crumbs in bottom of prepared pan, then pour in the butter, sugar, and egg mixture. Whip heavy cream until stiff, adding sugar gradually. Fold in crushed pineapple, spread over batter, and sprinkle with remaining wafer crumbs. Refrigerate 24 hours. Serves 16.

PUDDINGS

INVERARY INN

THE INN

INN AT CASTLE HILL

STEAMED CRANBERRY PUDDING

INVERARY INN, Baddeck, Nova Scotia, Canada

This inn on the Cabot Trail in Cape Breton, Nova Scotia, is famous for its home-cooked food. It's a real Scottish inn named for a famous castle. This is a very old Cape Breton recipe—and a great favorite at Inverary.

1 1/3 cup flour
pinch salt
1/2 cup molasses
1 tsp. baking powder
1/2 cup boiling water
2 scant tsp. baking soda
1 cup fresh cranberries

Grease a 4-cup steamed-pudding mold. In a large bowl combine flour, salt, molasses, and baking powder. In a small bowl pour boiling water over baking soda. Combine with molasses mixture. Add cranberries and mix well, transfer to prepared mold. Steam 1 1/2 hours. Serve warm with rum sauce. Serves 4.

RUM SAUCE:

1/2 cup sugar
1/2 cup heavy cream
1/4 cup butter
Rum or other flavoring to
taste

In a double boiler combine all ingredients and heat through. Serve hot.

FLAN

THE INN, Rancho Santa Fe, California

This elegant inn among orange groves, a short distance from San Diego, has been in the same family for many years. Gardens and eucalyptus trees make it a semi-tropical paradise.

1 3/4 cup sugar
1/2 cup water
1 qt. half-&-half, scalded
1 tsp. vanilla extract
8 egg yolks
pinch of salt

Preheat oven to 325°. To make the caramel, in a small saucepan combine the water and 1 cup of the sugar and cook the syrup until it becomes dark brown. Pour caramel into 8 individual flan or custard molds and turn the mold to coat the sides. Cool the caramel. Meanwhile, add the vanilla to the scalded half-&-half and cool slightly. To make the custard, beat the egg yolks with the remaining 3/4 cup sugar and the pinch of salt until the yolks are pale yellow. Add the half-&-half mixture. Strain the custard into the molds, then place them in a pan of simmering water. Bake 20 to 25 minutes, or until the flan is set. Chill at least 4 hours. Dip in hot water to unmold. Serves 8.

MOCHA MOUSSE

INN AT CASTLE HILL, Newport, Rhode Island

"Romantic" might be one of the best words to describe this inn which is located at the point where Narragansett Bay flows into the Atlantic Ocean. It is particularly exciting during the squalls and storms of September, October, and November. This would be a distinctive dessert for the most elegant dinner party.

1/2 lb. unsweetened
  baking chocolate, plus
   shaved chocolate for
    topping
1/3 cup water
1 dozen eggs, separated
1/2 cup instant coffee
3 cups sugar
6 tbsp. Kahlua
2 tbsp. Tia Maria
2 tbsp. coffee brandy
2 tbsp. Creme de Cacao
4 cups heavy cream
1 tbsp. vanilla extract

In a small saucepan melt the chocolate and water over low heat; set aside.

In a large mixing bowl, beat the egg yolks until lemon colored, then gradually add the instant coffee, 1 cup of the sugar, the chocolate, and the liqueurs, reserving 2 tablespoons of the Kahlua. In a separate bowl, beat the egg whites until they are stiff, gradually adding 1 cup of the sugar. Carefully fold the egg whites into the chocolate mixture, just until blended.

In another large mixing bowl, whip the heavy cream, the last cup of sugar, the remaining Kahlua, and the vanilla extract until the cream holds stiff peaks. Combine the chocolate mixture with the whipped cream, blending until smooth.

Transfer to individual 6-ounce serving dishes and top with shaved chocolate. Refrigerate immediately and serve chilled. Serves 16.

LEMON PUDDING

THREE VILLAGE INN, Stony Brook, New York

I enjoy a "lemony" dessert after a seafood dinner. Perhaps that's why I'm partial to this lemon pudding served at this inn located on the north shore of Long Island where exceptionally tasty seafood is served.

3 tbsp. butter, softened
1 cup sugar
2 tbsp. flour
juice and grated rind of
  one lemon
2 eggs, separated
1 cup milk

Preheat the oven to 350°. Beat the egg yolks until they are lemon colored. In a medium-sized mixing bowl, combine the butter, sugar, flour, lemon juice, grated lemon rind and milk, and add the beaten egg yolk. In a separate bowl beat the egg whites until stiff then fold them into the yolk mixture. Transfer to a shallow 8" baking dish and set into a pan of cold water. Bake 45 minutes or until a silver knife inserted into the center of the pudding comes out clean. Serve warm or cold. Serves 4.

ENGLISH PLUM PUDDING

LOWELL INN, Stillwater, Minnesota
It may be a long way from Piccadilly to Stillwater, Minnesota, but the Lowell Inn has successfully recreated the English scene with this typically British dessert. The Lowell is one of the most distinguished inns west of the Mississippi River and is famous for its unusually comfortable lodgings as well as its extensive menu.

2 lbs. raisins
1 lb. currants
1/4 lb. candied citron peel, chopped
1/4 lb. candied lemon peel, chopped
1/4 lb. blanched almonds, chopped
1 1/2 lbs. suet, chopped
1 1/2 cups flour
11 eggs, separated
1 1/4 cups brown sugar packed
4 cups bread crumbs
1/4 tsp. freshly grated nutmeg
1 1/2 tsp. ground cinnamon
1/4 tsp. ground cloves
1/2 tsp. salt
1/2 cup cider
4 tsp. vanilla extract
1/2 cup brandy

Line two 9x5x3" pans with linen. In a large mixing bowl combine fruits, nuts, and suet and dredge in flour. In another large mixing bowl beat the egg yolks until lemon colored; gradually add brown sugar, bread crumbs, spices, salt, cider, vanilla, and the dredged fruit and nuts. Finally, add the brandy. Beat the egg whites until fairly stiff but not too dry and fold into the fruit mixture. Divide fruit cake evenly between two lined pans and steam 8 hours. Top with Brandy Hard Sauce. Yield: Two 9x5x3" plum puddings.

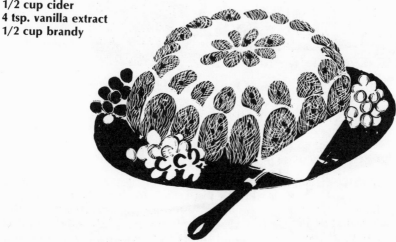

BRANDY HARD SAUCE:

2 1/2 cups butter, softened
8 cups confectioners sugar
2/3 cup brandy
2 tsp. vanilla extract

Cream butter, add powdered sugar gradually. Add brandy and vanilla last. The longer the beating the creamier the sauce.

WOODBOUND INN

WELSHFIELD INN

RALPH WALDO EMERSON

RICE PUDDING

WOODBOUND INN, Jaffrey, New Hampshire
Comfortably situated on the shores of a small lake, the Woodbound is a family-oriented resort-inn where many of the visitors have been returning year after year ever since the early 30s when the inn was founded. This rice pudding has been served to succeeding generations right from the start, and in many ways it is representative of the Woodbound's unpretentious but satisfying hospitality.

1/2 cup rice
2 cups milk
2 cups water
pinch of salt
1 cup sugar
3 eggs lightly beaten
1/2 tsp. vanilla
1/2 cup raisins
cinnamon

In a large, heavy, lidded saucepan, combine rice, milk, water, and salt, and simmer, covered. Meanwhile in a medium-sized mixing bowl combine remaining ingredients. When the rice is soft and has absorbed all the liquids, after about 35 minutes, pour egg mixture into the rice and combine thoroughly. Cook uncovered over low heat 5 minutes. Pour into a pan and top with a sprinkling of cinnamon. This may be prepared in and served from a chafing dish. Serves 6.

OLD-FASHIONED BREAD PUDDING

WELSHFIELD INN, Burton, Ohio
It was 1972 when I first found my way to this attractive restaurant in the heartland of Ohio. Brian and Polly Holmes have a reputation for fine food that extends far beyond the borders of their state. In addition, the Welshfield Inn is the only one where I have found a real honest-to-goodness nickelodeon.

4 cups milk, scalded
4 cups coarse dry bread
   crumbs
1/4 cup butter, melted
4 eggs, slightly beaten
1/2 cup seedless raisins
1/3 cup sugar
1/4 tsp. salt
1/2 tsp. freshly grated
   nutmeg
1/2 tsp. ground cinnamon
1 pt. vanilla ice cream
   (optional)

Preheat oven to 350°. Grease an 8x12" cake pan. In a large mixing bowl, pour milk over bread crumbs. In a small mixing bowl, combine all remaining ingredients and add to bread and milk mixture. Mix thoroughly, and pour into prepared cake pan. Bake 40 minutes or until a knife inserted into center of pudding comes out clean. Cut into squares and serve hot with a small scoop of vanilla ice cream, if desired. Serves 12.

GREAT NEW ENGLAND PUDDING

RALPH WALDO EMERSON, Rockport, Massachusetts

The porch of this inn with its massive Doric columns has a view that extends far out to sea and includes the only twin lighthouses on the New England coast. The inn has a reputation for hospitality that extends backward in time to the 19th century. Oddly enough, it consists of two buildings that were once at least two miles apart, but are now joined in one harmonious whole.

8 1/2 cups milk
5 shredded wheat biscuits
5 eggs
1 1/4 cup sugar
1 1/4 cup molasses
1 tsp. salt
1 tsp. ground cinnamon
1 tsp. ground nutmeg

Preheat oven to 275°. In a large bowl, pour 2 1/2 cups of the milk over the shredded wheat biscuits and set aside until the milk is absorbed. In another large bowl, beat the eggs and stir in remaining ingredients, mixing thoroughly. Combine with the shredded wheat mixture. Transfer to a 13x9x2" pan and bake 2 hours or until an inserted knife comes out clean. Serves 12.

PIES

DANA PLACE INN

BOTSFORD INN

BOULDERS INN

We have so many recipes calling for either baked or unbaked pie shells, we are providing herewith recipes for a plain crust and a graham cracker crust.

FLAKY PASTRY FOR 2-CRUST PIE (8 or 9")
(Cut in half for 1-crust pie)

2 cups sifted all-purpose flour
1 tsp. salt
3/4 cup shortening or 2/3 cup lard
4 to 5 tbsp. ice water

Sift flour with salt into medium bowl. With pastry blender, cut in shortening until mixture resembles coarse cornmeal. Quickly sprinkle ice water, 1 tablespoon at a time, over all of mixture, tossing lightly with a fork after each addition and pushing dampened portion to side of bowl; sprinkle only dry portion remaining. (Pastry should be just moist enough to hold together, not sticky.)

(If not for immediate use, shape pastry into a ball; wrap in waxed paper and refrigerate until ready to use. A 1-crust pie shell can be rolled out and fitted into a pie plate, and then refrigerated for future use.)

To make bottom crust: On lightly floured surface, roll out half of pastry to an 11-inch circle. Folding pastry in half, place fold at center of pie plate and unfold, fitting into plate. Press gently with fingertips to eliminate air bubbles.

For a 2-crust pie, trim even with edge of pie plate. For a 1-crust pie, fold under edge of crust and press into upright rim; crimp.

To bake 1-crust pie: Prick entire surface evenly with fork. Refrigerate 30 minutes. Meanwhile, preheat oven to 450°. Bake pie shell 8 to 10 minutes or until golden-brown.

For top crust of 2-crust pie: After rolling into 11" circle, cut vents for steam near center of pastry. Place pastry circle over filled pie. Trim crust 1/2" beyond edge of pie plate. Fold top crust under bottom crust, pressing the two together. Crimp edges. To prevent edge of crust from becoming too brown, place 1 1/2-inch strip of foil around crust; remove foil last 15 minutes of baking. Bake as recipe indicates.

UNBAKED GRAHAM CRACKER PIE SHELL (9")

1 1/3 cups graham cracker
crumbs (about 19
crackers)
1/4 cup soft butter or
margarine
1/4 cup sugar
1/4 tsp. cinnamon

Combine all ingredients in medium bowl; blend with fingers, fork, or pastry blender. Press evenly on bottom and side of 9-inch pie plate, not on rim. Refrigerate until ready to fill.

(To bake: Preheat oven to 375°. Bake 8 minutes or until golden brown. Cool on wire rack before filling.)

BLACK BOTTOM PIE

HOLLOWAY HOUSE, East Bloomfield, New York
Folks out in this part of New York State think absolutely nothing of traveling miles for a piece of this scrumptious Black Bottom Pie, which is a special Sunday treat.

1 8" baked, warm, pie crust
1/3 cup grated semisweet
chocolate
3 tbsp. cornstarch
1 tbsp. flour
1/4 cup sugar
1/2 cup milk, plus 1 1/2
cups milk, scalded
2 eggs, separated
1 tsp. butter
1 tsp. vanilla extract

While pie crust is still warm, sprinkle it with chocolate.

Prepare filling: In a small mixing bowl, combine cornstarch, flour, and sugar with 1/2 cup of the milk. In a medium-sized saucepan, combine the cornstarch mixture with the scalded milk. Beat the egg yolks. Add some of the hot mixture to the egg yolks, then pour the egg yolk mixture into the remaining contents of the saucepan. Cook, stirring constantly, until the custard has thickened. Remove from heat, stir in butter and vanilla. Beat egg whites until stiff, then fold into filling. Chill. Meanwhile, prepare the topping.

TOPPING:

2 egg whites
1/4 cup sugar
3/4 cup light corn syrup
1/4 tsp. salt
1 tsp. vanilla extract
grated semisweet chocolate

In a medium-sized bowl, beat egg whites until frothy. Add sugar and beat until mixture forms soft peaks. Add corn syrup, salt, and vanilla. Continue to beat until topping forms stiff peaks.

To assemble the pie: Pour filling over grated chocolate in pie crust. Spread topping on filling and sprinkle with grated chocolate. Yield: One 9" pie.

SPRINGSIDE INN

HOLLOWAY HOUSE

INN AT STARLIGHT LAKE

BRAZILIAN COURT

THE RED FOX TAVERN

HOLLYMEAD

KEY LIME PIE

BRAZILIAN COURT, Palm Beach, Florida
This is the "other side of Palm Beach"—not the side with the glittering social facade, but the side with more genuine people. This lovely conservative hotel has simplicity and good taste that will never go out of style. This recipe is one of the house favorites—Manager Bright Johnson says, "I believe you will find this quite delightful."

1 tbsp. gelatin
1/4 tsp. salt
1 cup sugar
1/2 cup fresh lime juice
1 tsp. finely grated lime rind
1/4 cup water
4 eggs, separated
2 cups heavy cream, whipped
3 drops green food coloring
1 9" baked pie shell

In a small saucepan, combine gelatin, salt, 1/2 cup of the sugar, lime juice, water, and egg yolks and cook until mixture comes to a boil. Cool custard until it begins to set. Meanwhile beat egg whites until they are stiff, gradually adding the remaining 1/2 cup sugar. Fold in 1 cup of the whipped cream, then fold the custard into the whipped cream mixture. Color slightly with food coloring. Pour filling into the pie crust and refrigerate for 2 hours. Top the pie with the remaining cup of whipped cream. Yield: One 9" pie.

BOURBON APPLE PIE

THE RED FOX TAVERN, Middleburg, Virginia
This two-hundred-year-old inn located in Virginia's horse country once had a visit from Confederate cavalryman Jeb Stuart. This apple pie with a little extra surprise would have persuaded him to linger longer.

1/2 cup raisins
bourbon—enough to cover raisins, plus 2 tbsp. bourbon
pastry for one 9" two-crust pie
3/4 cup sugar
2 tbsp. flour
1 tsp. ground cinnamon
1/8 tsp. nutmeg
1/4 tsp. salt
6 cups Winesap or cooking apples
1/2 cup toasted pecans or walnuts
2 tsp. apricot jelly
1 tbsp. butter
milk
sugar

To plump raisins soak in bourbon to cover for several hours or overnight. Cut apples into 1/4" slices and steam in small amount of water. Preheat oven to 425°. Line a greased 9" pie tin with 1/2 pastry dough. Combine sugar, flour, cinnamon, nutmeg, and salt. In another large bowl mix apples and the 2 tablespoons of bourbon. Add sugar mixture, pecans or walnuts, and raisins to apples, mix thoroughly. Paint bottom of pastry-lined pie tin with apricot jelly. Heap apple mixture in pastry. Dot with butter. Roll remaining pastry, place on top of apples, Flute edges, and cut vents in top of pastry. Brush top crust with milk and dust with sugar. Bake in lower third of oven, 50 to 60 minutes, or until crust is brown and apples tender. Yield: One 9" pie.

CRANBERRY TORTE PIE

DANA PLACE INN, Jackson, New Hampshire

New Hampshire's magnificent White Mountains and the rushing waters of the Ellis River combine to form an ideal backdrop for this warm friendly inn. Guests enjoy downhill and cross-country skiing in winter and the magnificent presence of Mount Washington in all seasons.

8 oz. fresh or frozen
  cranberries
1/2 cup chopped walnuts
1 1/2 cups sugar
2 eggs, beaten
3/4 cup flour
1/2 cup butter, melted

Preheat oven to 350°. Grease a 9" pie plate. Place cranberries in pie plate. Mix together chopped walnuts and 1/2 cup of the sugar. Cover cranberries with walnut mixture. In a medium-sized bowl, combine the remaining cup sugar, beaten eggs, and flour. Stir in melted butter and cover contents of pie plate with egg mixture. Bake 1 hour or until golden brown. Yield: One 9" torte pie.

MOCHA-TOFFEE PIE

HARBOR HOUSE, Elk, California

Since my first visit here in 1975, I have continued to be impressed with the exceptional view from the front desk and dining room of the offshore rocks and caverns, and with the wide variety and excellence of Patricia Corcoran's menu.

Note: Be sure to allow extra time for the various periods of refrigeration required for the filling and the topping on this pie.

PIE SHELL:

1/2 recipe for one 9" pie
1/4 cup firmly packed light
  brown sugar
3/4 cup finely chopped
  walnuts
1/2 square (1/2 oz.)
  unsweetened chocolate,
  grated
1 tsp. vanilla extract
1 tbsp. cold water

Preheat oven to 350°. Grease a 9" pie tin. In a large bowl and with your hands, thoroughly combine all ingredients. Press the dough firmly against bottom and sides of prepared pie tin. Bake 15 minutes. Cool. Meanwhile, prepare the filling.

FILLING:

2 tsp. crushed instant
  coffee
1/2 square (1/2 oz.)
  unsweetened chocolate,
  melted
1/2 cup butter, softened
3/4 cup sugar
2 eggs

Combine coffee and melted chocolate. Cool. In a small bowl, with mixer at medium speed, beat butter until creamy and fluffy. Gradually add sugar, beating until light. Blend in chocolate mixture. Add one of the eggs, beating at medium speed 5 minutes. Add remaining egg and beat 5 minutes longer. Pour into baked pie shell. Refrigerate, covered, several hours. Meanwhile, prepare the topping.

TOPPING:

1 cup heavy cream
2 tsp. instant coffee
1/4 cup confectioners
sugar
milk chocolate curls

In a small bowl, thoroughly combine cream, coffee, and confectioners sugar. Cover and refrigerate 1 hour.

·To assemble the pie: Beat topping mixture until stiff. Decorate pie with topping, sprinkling top with chocolate curls. Refrigerate 2 hours before serving. Yield: One 9" pie.

EGGNOG PIE

BOTSFORD INN, Farmington, Michigan

This inn in the Detroit suburbs was once the first stop on the stagecoach route leading to northern Michigan. Henry Ford restored it during the early 1920s, and there are ancient farm tools and other memorabilia of the 19th century adorning the walls of its sitting rooms. It may possibly be the oldest inn in Michigan.

1 8" baked pie shell
2 cups milk
3/4 cup sugar, plus 2 tbsp.
sugar
pinch of salt
4 egg yolks, plus 2 egg
whites
2 tbsp. cornstarch
3 tbsp. rum
1/2 cup cream, whipped
1/2 tsp. ground nutmeg

In a double boiler heat milk, the 3/4 cup of sugar, and salt until hot. In a small bowl combine egg yolks and cornstarch, beating well. Add yolks to hot milk mixture, adding the rum. Cook until mixture thickens, stirring occasionally. In another small bowl, beat the 2 egg whites with the 2 tablespoons of sugar until stiff, and fold into custard. Pour into pie shell and refrigerate for 2 hours or until thoroughly chilled. To serve, top with whipped cream and sprinkle with nutmeg. Yield: One 8" pie.

PECAN PIE

SPRINGSIDE INN, Auburn, New York

This is a family-run inn on the shores of Owasco Lake in the heart of New York State's Finger Lake Country. For many years, the inn featured dinner theater during the summer months. The cozy bedrooms, some of which overlook the duck pond in the front, are furnished like a central New York State sampler. Innkeeper Bill Dove says, "Don't count the calories on this one!"

12 eggs, lightly beaten
1 1/3 cups sugar
4 cups corn syrup
16 tbsp. butter (1/2 lb.)
4 tsp. vanilla extract
1/2 tsp. salt
4 tsp. lemon juice
4 cups pecan halves
three 9" pie shells
whipped cream

Preheat oven to 350°. Combine all ingredients except pecans and whipped cream. Fold in pecans. Pour mixture into pie shells. Bake 50 minutes. Serve with fresh whipped cream. Yield: Three 9" pies.

SOUR CREAM APPLE PIE

INN AT STARLIGHT LAKE, Starlight, Pennsylvania
Rambling, old-fashioned, and comfortable, this inn is situated on a back road in the rolling hills of northeastern Pennsylvania. A great place for families, with many diversions for children.

2 tbsp. flour, plus 1/3 cup
  flour for topping
pinch salt
3/4 cup sugar
1 egg
1 cup sour cream or sour
  milk
1 tsp. vanilla extract
1/4 tsp. freshly grated
  nutmeg
2 cups peeled, diced or
  shredded apples
1 9" unbaked pie shell
1/4 cup butter, softened
1/3 cup firmly packed
  brown sugar
1 tsp. ground cinnamon

Preheat oven to 400°. In a medium-sized bowl, combine the two tablespoons of flour, salt, and sugar. Add, and combine thoroughly, egg, sour cream or sour milk, vanilla, and nutmeg. Fold in the diced or shredded apples. Pour the smooth, thin batter into pie crust. Bake 15 minutes, then reduce oven temperature to 350° and bake 30 minutes longer. Meanwhile, in a small bowl, combine butter, brown sugar, remaining 1/3 cup flour and cinnamon. Sprinkle brown sugar mixture onto pie. Increase oven temperature to 400° and bake the pie 10 minutes longer or until golden brown. Yield: One 9" pie.

LEMON PIE

BOULDERS INN, New Preston, Connecticut
This warm, comfortable resort-inn on Lake Waramaug offers an endless variety of activities for both summer and winter, with boats, tennis courts, and woodland trails for walking or skiing.

MERINGUE CRUST:

4 egg whites
1/4 tsp. cream of tartar
1 cup sugar

Preheat oven to 250°. Grease a deep 9-inch pie dish. Beat egg whites until foamy; add cream of tartar and, gradually incorporating sugar, continue beating until egg whites are stiff. Bake 1 hour or until meringue crust is dry. Meanwhile prepare filling.

FILLING:

4 egg yolks
1/2 cup sugar
3 tbsp. lemon juice
1 tbsp. grated lemon peel
1 cup heavy cream,
  whipped

Beat egg yolks until thick and lemon colored; gradually add sugar, lemon juice, and peel. Transfer to a double boiler and cook until filling is thickened. Cool.

To assemble the pie: Fill crust with lemon custard; top with whipped cream. Refrigerate overnight. Yield: One 9" pie.

O-SO-GOOD PIE

ALEXANDER-WITHROW HOUSE, Lexington, Virginia
This exquisite guest house was built in 1789 and is in the National Register of Historic Places. It is one of the few structures to survive a disastrous fire in Lexington in 1796. This area, of course, is saturated with landmarks of historical interest.

1 cup sugar
1 tbsp. butter, melted
2 tbsp. cider vinegar
1 tbsp. water
1/2 tsp. ground cloves
1/2 tsp. ground cinnamon
1/2 cup raisins
1/4 cup chopped nuts
2 eggs, beaten
1 9" unbaked pie crust

Preheat oven to 350°. In a medium-sized bowl, combine all filling ingredients, adding eggs last. Pour into unbaked pie crust. Bake 30 minutes, or until crisp golden brown crust is formed. Yield: One 9" pie.

INNKEEPER'S PIE

THE BRADLEY INN, New Harbor, Maine
Pemaquid Point Light, built in 1827, still stands guard over Muscongus Bay just a very short walking distance from The Bradley Inn. This 70-year-old building has been restored with loving care and now offers a real country inn experience with pleasantly decorated rooms. The area abounds in history and wonderful year-round recreational opportunities.

One 10" pie shell (below)
3 eggs
1 1/2 cups sugar
3/4 cup light corn syrup
1 1/4 cups uncooked oatmeal
1 1/4 cups shredded or flaked coconut
6 oz. canned evaporated milk
6 tbsp. melted margarine
1/2 cup whipped cream

Prepare pie shell. Preheat oven to 400°. In a large bowl lightly beat eggs. Add all other ingredients and mix until well blended. Pour into unbaked pie shell. Bake for 20 minutes. Lower oven setting to 250° and bake 45 to 50 minutes or until pie is set and center is firm. Cool. Cover with whipped cream just before serving. Yield: One 10" pie.

PASTRY:

1 3/4 cups pre-sifted flour
3/4 tsp. salt
3/4 cup shortening
4 tbsp. ice water

In a medium-sized bowl combine flour and salt. Cut in shortening with pastry blender. Sprinkle with water, 1 tablespoon at a time, mixing with a fork until flour is moistened and will hold together in a ball. Roll out on floured surface and line a 10" pie plate.

PEANUT BUTTER CREAM PIE

LAKESIDE INN, Mt. Dora, Florida

Mt. Dora is like a New England town in the middle of Florida. When this delicious concoction is on the menu, the Lakeside always has many requests for seconds. In fact, it's so good we're giving the recipe for two pies!

1/2 cup peanut butter
3/4 cup confectioners
  sugar
2 unbaked 9" pie crusts
1/2 cup flour
3/4 cup sugar
2 cups milk, scalded
1/8 tsp. salt
4 eggs, separated
1 tsp. vanilla extract
2 tbsp. butter, softened
1 tsp. cream of tartar
2 tbsp. cornstarch

Preheat the oven to 350°. In a small mixing bowl, combine the peanut butter and confectioners sugar to make fine crumbs. Place half of the peanut butter crumbs in the bottom of the prepared pie crusts. In a medium-sized bowl, combine the flour, sugar, milk, salt, egg yolks, vanilla, and butter and pour this filling over the peanut butter crumbs. Beat the egg whites until stiff, gradually adding the cream of tartar and cornstarch. Place this meringue over the filled pies. Top with remaining peanut butter crumbs. Bake 15 to 20 minutes. Yield: Two 9" pies.

LIME PARFAIT PIE

HOLLYMEAD, Charlottesville, Virginia

This country restaurant in a building of great historic interest is located just a few miles north of the University of Virginia in Charlottesville. Besides this dish, innkeeper Peg Bute also features Beef Wellington, trout stuffed with crabmeat, flounder with shrimp, and country stuffed pork chops.

1 6-oz. package lime-
  flavored gelatin
2 cups boiling water
1 tsp. grated lime peel
1/3 cup lime juice
1 qt. vanilla ice cream
1 baked 9" pie crust, or
  1 9" graham cracker crust
whipped cream for topping
maraschino cherries for
  garnish

Dissolve gelatin in boiling water. Stir in lime juice and peel. Add ice cream by spoonfuls, stirring until melted. Chill until mixture mounds. Pile into pie shell. Chill until firm. Top with whipped cream and maraschino cherries. Yield: One 9" pie.

DESSERTS
AND SAUCES

THE HAWTHORNE INN

SUTTER CREEK INN

THE OVERLOOK INN

WILD BLACKBERRY TURNOVERS

THE HAWTHORNE INN, Concord, Massachusetts

A charming, small village inn with a young and versatile innkeeper, Gregory Burch, who has carefully and patiently restored it room by room to its original colonial style. Although a Continental breakfast is the only meal offered, guests are regaled with fresh-baked rolls, heaps of butter and jam, fruit juices, and delicious coffee. Concord, of course, is full of historic points of interest.

DOUGH:

1/4 cup honey
1/2 cup butter, softened
2 eggs
1 tsp. vanilla extract
2 1/2 cups Cornell mix
   (below)
2 tsp. baking powder
1/2 tsp. salt

In a large mixing bowl, cream together the honey and butter until they are light and fluffy; then, one at a time, beat in the eggs. Add vanilla. In a separate, medium-sized bowl, combine Cornell mix, baking powder, and salt. Gradually add to the butter mixture, beating well after each addition. Continue to beat until the dough is smooth. Chill. Meanwhile, prepare the filling.

CORNELL MIX:

2 tbsp., plus 1 1/2 tsp. soy
   flour
2 tbsp., plus 1 1/2 tsp.
   powdered milk
2 tbsp., plus 1 1/2 tsp. bran
2 tbsp., plus 1 1/2 tsp. rye
   flour
2 tbsp., plus 1 1/2 tsp. wheat
   germ
unbleached flour

In a 1-quart measuring cup, combine all ingredients except flour; then add sufficient flour to prepare 2 1/2 cups mix.

FILLING:

1 qt. fresh blackberries
2 tbsp. butter, melted
1 tsp. ground cinnamon,
   plus ground cinnamon
   for topping
firmly packed brown sugar
1 tbsp. flour
sugar for topping

In a medium-sized bowl, combine blackberries, melted butter, one teaspoon of the cinnamon, brown sugar to taste, and flour.

To assemble the turnovers: Preheat oven to 400°. Lightly grease two baking sheets. When dough is sufficiently stiff to handle, transfer it to a floured board and roll to a thickness of 1/4 inch. Cut dough into eighteen 4" circles. Place a heaping tablespoon of filling on half of each circle. Fold unfilled portion of dough over blackberry mixture. Firmly pinch edges of each turnover and pierce top with a fork. Dust with cinnamon and sugar. Transfer to prepared baking sheets and bake 15 minutes, or until golden. Yield: 18 turnovers.

COFFEE PARFAIT

SUTTER CREEK INN, Sutter Creek, California
This is a typical New Hampshire Inn with its white picket fence—but it's in northern California in the middle of the gold rush country! Jane Way makes a visit here a very special experience.

1/2 lb. marshmallows,
  chopped
pinch salt
4 cups hot coffee
1/3 cup brandy
1 cup heavy cream,
  whipped

Melt marshmallows with salt in hot coffee. Pour brandy over marshmallow mixture and allow it to seep through. Top with whipped cream. Chill. Serves 4.

PENNSYLVANIA PEACHES

THE OVERLOOK INN, Canadensis, Pennsylvania
Many people love to spend Christmas at this comfortable inn among the pine-scented forests of the Poconos. Lolly and Bob Tupper make it a real occasion with handmade and old-fashioned ornaments, special candles, and pine sprays and wreaths everywhere. There are many outdoor activities here both summer and winter.

6 fresh or home-canned
  chilled peaches, peeled
  and sliced
1 cup whipped cream
confectioners sugar, to taste
1 tbsp. brandy
2 cups Crème Patissière
  (below)
freshly grated nutmeg

To serve, place peach slices in a circle in 6 individual serving dishes. Sweeten whipped cream to taste with confectioners sugar and add brandy. Pour 1/3 cup Crème Patissière over each portion of peaches. Place two heaping tablespoons whipped cream over peaches and Crème. Sprinkle with nutmeg. Serve very cold. Serves 6.

CRÈME PATISSIÈRE:

1 1/2 cups heavy cream
1/2 cup milk
6 egg yolks
2/3 cup sugar
4 tbsp. brandy
1/2 cup flour

In a 2-quart saucepan, bring cream and milk to a boil. Set aside to cool. In a medium-sized mixing bowl, combine egg yolks, sugar and brandy; whisk until mixture drops from the whisk in a ribbon. Add flour and mix well. Pour 1/2 the hot mixture into the egg yolk mixture, combining thoroughly; then pour into the remaining hot cream and milk. Over medium heat, stirring constantly, bring to a boil—at which point the mixture will thicken; lower heat and cook 2 or 3 minutes longer, continuing to stir constantly to prevent scorching. Chill until ready to serve.

HEAVENLY DELIGHT

THE YANKEE CLIPPER, Rockport, Massachusetts

This seacoast inn is on the north shore of Massachusetts, about one hour from Boston. Rockport is well-known as an artist's colony, and a combination of massive rocks and fishing boats which are visible from the porches and lawns of the Yankee Clipper have been painted many times.

1 13 oz. can evaporated milk
1 box lemon-flavored gelatine
Grated rind and juice of 1 lemon
1 cup sugar
1 package lady fingers
1/2 cup whipped cream

Before starting this recipe, refrigerate the evaporated milk for 24 hours, and chill a medium-sized bowl and a beater.

In a large bowl dissolve gelatine in boiling water. Cool, but do not allow to set. Add lemon rind, lemon juice, and sugar. In chilled bowl, beat evaporated milk until stiff. Combine with gelatine mixture. Place a layer of lady fingers on bottom of flat dish. Spread with gelatine-milk mixture and cover with another layer of lady fingers. Add second layer of gelatine-milk mixture, and cool until set. Top with whipped cream. Serves 6 to 8.

LEMON SHERBET

MARSHLANDS INN, Sackville, New Brunswick, Canada

Innkeepers Herb and Alice Read are continuing a family tradition at this inn which is on the road to Prince Edward Island as well as to Nova Scotia. The dinnerware is sterling, the china is Spode and all the waitresses wear dark blue uniforms with white collars and aprons. This recipe is one of the specialties of the house.

1 qt. lemon juice (juice of 18 to 20 lemons), plus finely grated peel of 8 lemons
6 cups sugar
1 pt. heavy cream
milk

In a large mixing bowl, combine lemon juice and peel. Stirring, dissolve sugar in juice. Stir in cream and add sufficient milk to fill a 2-gallon ice cream freezer to within 4 inches of top. Freeze the old-fashioned way with ice and salt. Yield: 2 gallons sherbet.

FROZEN HICKORY STICKS

HICKORY STICK FARM, Laconia, New Hampshire

Visiting this old converted farmhouse restaurant on a hilltop can be an adventure on the back roads of the lake country of New Hampshire—and when you get there, don't forget they are noted for their roast duckling. We tried to pin down Mary and Scott Roeder on exactly how many of these scrumptious Hickory Sticks this recipe makes, but it seems there are so many possible sizes, that the best we can do is to say there'll be plenty for everybody and you can have a lot of fun making and eating them!

Cookie Crumbs (below)
vanilla ice cream
Hot Fudge Sauce (below)
chopped nuts for garnish

To make the Hickory Sticks, spread Cookie Crumbs in a layer on a marble slab, formica counter, or bread board. Place a scoop of vanilla ice cream over the crumbs and roll into the shape of a log. The ice cream must be just softened, neither too hard nor too soft, or rolling will be difficult. Rolled Hickory Sticks may be made ahead and stored in the freezer.

To serve the Hickory Sticks, place a spoonful of Hot Fudge Sauce in center of plate, top with a Hickory Stick and garnish with chopped nuts.

COOKIE CRUMBS:

2 1/2 cups sugar
1 lb. shortening
7 cups flour
2 1/2 tbsp. baking powder
1/2 tsp. salt
1/4 cup milk
3 eggs
1 tbsp. vanilla extract
8 oz. bakers (bitter)
    chocolate, melted

In a large mixing bowl, cream together until light and fluffy the sugar and shortening. In a separate bowl, mix together the flour, baking powder and salt. In a third bowl combine the milk, eggs and vanilla. Alternating a small amount of each, add the dry ingredients, liquids and chocolate to the creamed shortening. Shape the dough into rolls, wrap in waxed paper and refrigerate at least one day.

Preheat the oven to 375°. Slice the rolls of dough and bake the cookies 8 to 10 minutes. Cool until crisp, then grind into crumbs with a rolling pin or grater attachment of mixer. Crumbs may be made in advance and stored in a covered canister.

HOT FUDGE SAUCE:

1/4 lb. margarine
1 13-oz. can evaporated
    milk
1 lb. confectioners sugar
8 oz. bakers (bitter)
    chocolate
1 tsp. vanilla extract

In the top of the double boiler, combine and heat until melted the margarine, evaporated milk, confectioners sugar and chocolate. Add vanilla and whip vigorously until smooth. This sauce keeps very well in a tightly covered container in refrigerator.

HICKORY STICK FARM

THE YANKEE CLIPPER

MARSHLANDS INN

OLD CLUB RESTAURANT

ELMWOOD INN

MORRILL PLACE

TIPSY PARSON

OLD CLUB RESTAURANT, Alexandria, Virginia
In a colonial mansion in the historic section of Alexandria, just across the river from Washington, D.C., the oldest part of this restaurant was built by George Washington and his friends as a private club. Genuine southern country cooking is featured here.

1 pound cake (16 oz.)
1 1/4 cup sherry
1 tbsp. unflavored gelatine
1/4 cup cold water
5 egg yolks, slightly beaten
1 cup sugar
1 1/2 cups milk
3 egg whites
whipped cream
slivered toasted almonds

Cut cake into 1" slices and line bottom of a 9x9x2" pan with the cake slices. Pour sherry evenly over the cake. Soften gelatine in water. Beat egg yolks with 1/2 cup sugar and set aside. Scald milk in double boiler, add gelatine and stir well. Add egg yolk mixture and continue to cook and stir until mixture coats spoon. Cover and cool slightly, then pour over sherried cake. Cool until jelled. Beat egg whites until frothy, add remaining sugar and beat until peak is formed. Spread over top of custard and serve with a dollop of whipped cream sprinkled with toasted almonds. Serves 10.

KENTUCKY BOURBON SAUCE

ELMWOOD INN, Perryville, Kentucky
The Elmwood Inn could happen only in Kentucky. Surrounded by a grove of maple and sweetgum trees beside the Chaplin River, the inn features traditional southern dishes in an atmosphere of Greek Revival elegance. Southern fried chicken with cream gravy, freshly made hot biscuits filled with Kentucky fried ham, fresh fruit salads, and the like will be enjoyed by guests of this country restaurant.

1 cup sugar
1/4 cup butter
1 small can evaporated
  milk
1 egg
1/4 cup Kentucky
  bourbon whiskey

In a double boiler combine all ingredients except whiskey, and cook over low heat until sauce has begun to thicken. Remove from heat and cool. When the sauce is cool add the whiskey and beat with an electric mixer until smooth. Serve over ice cream, plum pudding, or fruit cake. Yield: 1 1/2 cups. This sauce will keep for weeks in the refrigerator.

GRANDMA OIE'S FUDGE SAUCE

MORRILL PLACE, Newburyport, Massachusetts
Built in 1806, this is one of the famous mansions on Newburyport's High Street, which is one of the best preserved areas of early New England. Its former owners included three Newburyport sea captains, and it boasts a widow's walk. Innkeeper Rose Ann Hunter persuaded her husband Paul's grandmother to part with this treasured recipe.

4 1-oz. squares unsweetened chocolate
2 tbsp. butter
1 1/2 cups sugar
6 tbsp. milk
salt to taste
dash vanilla extract
2 eggs

In a double boiler melt chocolate and butter. Add sugar, milk, salt, and vanilla, whisking until sauce is slightly thickened. Cool. Add eggs and stir. Best when made ahead. To serve, heat in double boiler until thick. Serves 8.

CONDIMENTS
AND JAMS

MOUNTAIN VIEW INN

RED INN RESTAURANT

JAMES HOUSE

PEAR BUTTER

PARTRIDGE INN, Underwood, Washington

A modest, unassuming restaurant with two lodging rooms and spectacular views of the Columbia River and surrounding mountains and valleys. Nora McNab's joy in innkeeping and cooking shows in her delicious meals. Here's what she serves with her homemade breads.

1 1-gallon can pears, drained, juice reserved
red food coloring
2 cups sugar
1/4 cup lemon juice
1 tsp. ground cinnamon
pinch ground cloves
pinch freshly grated nutmeg
pinch allspice
pinch salt

Into a kettle, drain half the pear juice. Boil 10 minutes or until reduced by half. In a blender, purée pears with remaining juice and add to boiling juice. Simmer 1/2 hour, then add a few drops of red food coloring, sugar, lemon juice, and spices. Mix well and continue to simmer one hour longer. Serve immediately or refrigerate. If not for immediate use, pear butter should be sealed in sterilized pint jars and processed 10 minutes. Yield: 8 pints pear butter.

WATERMELON RIND PRESERVES

NU-WRAY INN, Burnsville, North Carolina

Here's a famous inn in the Great Smoky mountains where everybody is roused out of bed at 8 a.m. so that they can all sit down together at the long breakfast table at 8:30.

1 tbsp. slack lime (available at most pharmacies)
rind of one large watermelon, cubed and weighed
2 lbs. sugar for each pound rind
2 tbsp. chopped fresh ginger root
3 lemons, thinly sliced

In a large bowl, dissolve the lime in sufficient water to completely cover the melon rind. Soak rind overnight. Drain. Rinse thoroughly. Transfer rind to a large saucepan and cover with hot water. Add 2 pounds sugar for each pound rind. Boil several hours until rind is translucent and a thick syrup has formed, adding water as necessary to prevent syrup from crystalizing. Pour contents of saucepan into sterilized jars, adding the ginger and lemon and dividing them evenly among the jars. Process. Yield: 4 quarts preserves.

RHUBARB JAM

LAKE QUINALT LODGE, Lake Quinalt, Washington

The LQL is located in the famous rain forest of the Olympic Peninsula, to the west of Seattle. Although there are Douglas firs that reach high into the sky, with this recipe, the lowly rhubarb also achieves a well-deserved plaudit.

**2 lbs. ripe rhubarb, thinly
   sliced or chopped
3/4 cup water
5 1/2 cups sugar
3 oz. liquid fruit pectin**

In a 3-quart lidded saucepan, combine the rhubarb and water and simmer, covered, one minute or until the fruit is soft. Into another 3-quart saucepan measure 3 cups of the prepared fruit. Add the sugar and mix well. Over high heat, bring the fruit and sugar to a rolling boil and cook one minute, stirring constantly. Remove from the heat and stir in the liquid pectin. Skim off any foam with metal spoon. Stir and skim 5 minutes longer to prevent fruit from rising to the top of the jam. Ladle into sterilized glasses and immediately cover with 1/8″ hot paraffin. Yield: 6 1/4 cups (4 lbs.) jam.

JEAN'S RHUBARB CHUTNEY SAUCE

WHITEHALL INN, Camden, Maine

Chutney and rhubarb, what a combination! The guests at this Maine seacoast inn devour this condiment with gusto. The nice thing about it is that it's an easy-to-make preserve. Camden is one of Maine's picturesque seacoast towns.

**1 cup seedless raisins
1 cup finely chopped
   onion
8 cups coarsely chopped
   rhubarb
1/2 cup cider vinegar
2 cups firmly packed
   brown sugar
1 tsp. salt
1/2 tsp. ground cinnamon
1/2 tsp. ground ginger
1/2 tsp. allspice
grated rind of one orange**

In a large, heavy stockpot, combine all ingredients and bring to a boil; simmer 20 minutes, or until sauce is thick. To preserve: Process in sterilized jars. If chutney sauce is not preserved, you may add 1/2 cup chopped walnuts. Chutney sauce is good with pork, chicken, or lamb. Yield: 2 1/2 pints chutney sauce.

TASTY RELISH

RED INN RESTAURANT, Provincetown, Massachusetts
The striking view of Provincetown Harbor on Cape Cod, the fragrant wood fire in the huge hearth, and candlelit tables—not to mention the marvellous food—make this restaurant a very special place to dine.

6 cups red kidney beans, drained
6 hard-cooked eggs, chopped
2 medium onions, chopped
1 bunch celery, chopped
3 tbsp. mayonnaise
2 tbsp. dill relish
 (or substitute 2 tbsp. finely chopped dill pickle)
1 tbsp. curry powder
1 tsp. salt
3/4 tsp. white pepper

In a large mixing bowl, combine beans, eggs, onions, and celery. In a small bowl, combine mayonnaise, dill relish or chopped pickle, curry powder, salt, and white pepper and add to the first mixture, stirring thoroughly. Refrigerate. Yield: 8 cups relish.

MUSTARD PICKLES

MOUNTAIN VIEW INN, Norfolk, Connecticut
Located off the main street of this northwestern Connecticut village, the Mountain View Inn is just a short distance from the Yale University Summer School of Music. This section of Connecticut has many natural attractions, too, including cross-country ski trails, walking paths, and quiet back roads.

1 qt. cucumbers
1 qt. pickling cucumbers
1 qt. pearl onions
1 qt. green peppers, seeded and quartered
2 red peppers
1 head cauliflower, separated into flowerets
2 qts. water
1 cup salt
6 tbsp. dry mustard
1 tbsp. turmeric
1 3/4 cups flour
2 cups sugar
2 qts. white vinegar

Cut up vegetables in small chunks. Place vegetables in a large bowl. Combine water and salt and pour over the vegetables. Soak overnight at room temperature. In a large saucepan combine the remaining ingredients and boil until thick. In a separate large saucepan boil the vegetables until they are slightly tender. Drain the vegetables. Return the vegetables to the large saucepan, cover with the vinegar sauce and bring to a boil. Transfer to sterile jars and seal. Yield: Approximately 1 1/2 gallons.

ROSETREE JAM

JAMES HOUSE, Port Townsend, Washington
Plants, books, good music, comfortable reading areas, and some beautiful antiques are a few of the things that make this bed-and-breakfast Victorian mansion such a pleasure.

6 lbs. apricots, pitted and sliced
6 pts. raspberries or 4 10-oz. packages frozen raspberries, thawed
2 20-oz. cans crushed pineapple, drained
4 lbs. sugar

In a large saucepan, combine all ingredients. Bring to a boil and cook 30 minutes, stirring frequently. Seal in jars. Yield: 24 small jars.

ZUCCHINI EMERALD MARMALADE

HARTWELL HOUSE, Ogunquit, Maine
This elegant guest house is just a few steps from the Whistling Oyster and Perkins Cove. Although Hartwell House doesn't offer meals, Trisha Hartwell says that when she gets into the "country homemaking mood" she has made this marmalade and given it to her guests. For a finishing touch, she ties a green checked ribbon around each jar.

5 cups zucchini, coarsely shredded
2 1/2 cups water
5/8 cup fresh lime juice, plus 4 tbsp. grated lime peel
1 pkg. powdered fruit pectin (1 3/4 oz.)
5 1/4 cups sugar

In a 6-quart Dutch oven, combine all ingredients and bring to a boil. Boil gently for about 12 minutes. Stir in powdered pectin and return to a boil. Stir in sugar and lime peel and continue boiling. Liquid should be thick at this point and should be boiling rapidly. Stirring constantly, continue to boil for 2 minutes. Remove from heat and continue stirring for about 7 minutes. Pour into sterilized half-pint jelly glasses, seal. Yield: 6 half-pints marmalade.

INDEX OF INNS

Inn at Princeton, Princeton, Massachusetts
(Paupiettes de Veau aux Duxelles, Sauce Béarnaise), 82
Inn at Sawmill Farm, West Dover, Vermont
(Chocolate Cake), 121
Inn at Starlight Lake, Starlight, Pennsylvania
(Sour Cream Apple Cake), 144
Inn on the Common, Craftsbury Common, Vermont
(Cold Spaghetti Salad), 44
Inn on the Library Lawn, Westport, New York
(Tomato Pie), 93
Inverary Inn, Baddeck, Nova Scotia, Canada
(Steamed Cranberry Pudding), 129

James House, Port Townsend, Washington
(Rosetree Jam), 162
John Hancock Inn, Hancock, New Hampshire
(Cheesecake Doucette), 125

Kedron Valley Inn, South Woodstock, Vermont
(Chocolate Peppermint Cake), 120
Kilmuir Place, Northeast Margaree, Cape Breton, Nova Scotia
(Lobster au Gratin), 58

Lake Quinault Lodge, Quinault, Washington
(Rhubarb Jam), 160
Lakeside Inn, Mt. Dora, Florida
(Peanut Butter Cream Pie), 146
Larchwood Inn, Wakefield, Rhode Island
(Baked Flounder with Scallop Stuffing), 56
Lincklaen House, Cazenovia, New York
(Spinach Soufflé), 92
Lodge on the Desert, Tucson, Arizona
(French-Fried Turkey), 69
Longfellow's Wayside Inn, South Sudbury, Massachusetts
(Yankee Pot Roast), 82
Lovett's by Lafayette Brook, Franconia, New Hampshire
(Salmon Mousse), 25
Lowell Inn, Stillwater, Minnesota
(English Plum Pudding), 131
Lyme Inn, Lyme, New Hampshire
(Hasenpfeffer), 71

Mainstay Inn, Cape May, New Jersey
(Ground Beef Quiche), 100
Marathon Inn, North Head, Grand Manan Island, New Brunswick
(Lemon Mushroom Sauce for Fish), 64
Marshlands Inn, Sackville, New Brunswick
(Lemon Sherbet), 151
Maryland Inn, Annapolis, Maryland
(Crab Bisque), 35
Milford House, Annapolis Royal, Nova Scotia
(Scallop Casserole), 58

Millhof Inn, Stephentown, New York
(Goulash), 80
Morrill Place, Newburyport, Massachusetts
(Grandma Oie's Fudge Sauce), 156
Mountain View Inn, Norfolk, Connecticut
(Mustard Pickles), 161

Nauset House, East Orleans, Massachusetts
(Quiche Lorraine), 101
North Hero House, North Hero, Vermont
(Chablis Cheddar Cheese Soup), 39
Nu-Wray Inn, Burnsville, North Carolina
(Watermelon Rind Preserves), 159

Oban Inn, Niagara-on-the-Lake, Ontario, Canada
(Mongol Soup), 40
Old Club Restaurant, Alexandria, Virginia
(Tipsy Parson), 155
Old Drovers Inn, Dover Plains, New York
(Turkey Hash with Mustard Sauce), 103
Outlook Lodge, Green Mountain Falls, Colorado
(Gumdrop Bread), 108
Overlook Inn, Canadensis, Pennsylvania
(Pennsylvania Peaches), 150

Partridge Inn, Underwood, Washington
(Pear Butter), 159
Patchwork Quilt, Middlebury, Indiana
(Country House Dressing), 48
Pentagoet Inn, Castine, Maine
(Basil and Caper Sauce), 96
Philbrook Farm Inn, Shelburne, New Hampshire
(Dark Bread), 114
Peirson Place, Richmond, Massachusetts
(Thornoby Tea Torte), 122
Pilgrim's Inn, Deer Isle, Maine
(Joyous Strawberry Granita Cake), 118
Pine Barn Inn, Danville, Pennsylvania
(Pennsylvania Dutch-Style Chicken Pot Pie), 67
Prospect Hill Inn, Trevilians, Virginia
(Mireille's Salade Vinaigrette), 44
Pump House Inn, Canadensis, Pennsylvania
(Seviche of Scallops), 25

Ralph Waldo Emerson Inn, Rockport, Massachusetts
(Great New England Pudding), 134
Rancho de los Caballeros, Wickenburg, Arizona
(Cheese Enchiladas), 102
Red Fox Tavern, Middletown, Virginia
(Bourbon Apple Pie), 141
Red Inn, Provincetown, Massachusetts
(Tasty Relish), 161

Red Lion Inn, Stockbridge, Massachusetts
(Cioppino), 55
Redcoat's Return, Tannersville, New York
(Ham and Cheese Beignets), 23
Robert Morris Inn, Oxford, Maryland
(Cranberry Muffins), 107
Rockhouse Mountain Farm, Eaton Center, New Hampshire
(Blueberry Cake), 123

St. Gemme Beauvais Inn, Ste. Genevieve, Missouri
(French Crullers), 108
Schumacher's New Prague Hotel, New Prague, Minnesota
(Duck Liver Paste), 28
Sea Hut, Palmetto, Florida
(Crab Imperial), 27
1740 House, Lumberville, Pennsylvania
(Tia Maria Cake), 119
1770 House, East Hampton, New York
(Classic Oriental Dressing), 50
Shaw's Hotel, Brackley Point, Prince Edward Island, Canada
(Deviled Scallops), 59
Sherwood Inn, Skaneateles, New York
(Crabmeat and Avocado Quiche), 104
Silvermine Tavern, Norwalk, Connecticut
(Oysters Victoria), 54
1661 House, Block Island, Rhode Island
(Poulet au Citron), 70
Spalding Inn Club, Whitefield, New Hampshire
(Iced Lemon Soup), 35
Springside Inn, Auburn, New York
(Pecan Pie), 143
Squire Tarbox Inn, Wiscasset, Maine
(Poppy Seed Dressing), 50
Stafford's Bay View Inn, Petoskey, Michigan
(Tomato Pudding), 95
Stafford's in the Field, Chocorua, New Hampshire
(Lemon Puffs), 107
Stagecoach Hill Inn, Sheffield, Massachusetts
(Oyster Pie), 62
Sterling Inn, South Sterling, Pennsylvania
(Beef Stew with Homemade Baking Powder Biscuits), 78
Sutter Creek Inn, Sutter Creek, California
(Coffee Parfait), 150
Swiss Hutte, Hillsdale, New York
(Cute de Veau Normande), 77
Swordgate Inn, Charleston, South Carolina
(Cinnamon Flip), 126

Tanque Verde Ranch, Tucson, Arizona
(Cabrilla—Red Snapper), 54
Tavern, The, New Wilmington, Pennsylvania
(Sauerkraut and Baked Beans), 92

Three Village Inn, Stony Brook, New York
(Lemon Pudding), 130
Town Farms Inn, Middletown, Connecticut
(Chicken Hash), 101

Victorian Inn, Whitinsville, Massachusetts
(Fillet of Sole Stuffed with Salmon Mousse), 61
Village Inn, Landgrove, Vermont
(Bordelaise Sauce), 87
Village Inn, Lenox, Massachusetts
(Pineapple Icebox Cake), 126

Waterford Inne, East Waterford, Maine
(Zucchini Squares), 91
Wayside Inn, Middletown, Virginia
(Peanut Dressing), 74
Welshfield Inn, Burton, Ohio
(Old-Fashioned Bread Pudding), 133
Whistling Oyster, Ogunquit, Maine
(Crabmeat Snug Harbor), 59
White Gull Inn, Fish Creek, Wisconsin
(Fish Boil), 64
White Hart Inn, Salisbury, Connecticut
(Mandarin Sweet and Sour Pork), 79
Whitehall Inn, Camden, Maine
(Jean's Rhubarb Chutney Sauce), 160
Wilderness Lodge, Lesterville, Missouri
(Stuffed Pork Chops), 84
Windsor House, Newburyport, Massachusetts
(Tomato Soup), 39
Woodbound Inn, Jaffrey, New Hampshire
(Rice Pudding), 133

Yankee Clipper, Rockport, Massachusetts
(Heavenly Delight), 151

INDEX OF RECIPES